10 *Bizarre* Interview Glitches – BIG 10

BLUNDERS MADE DURING INTERVIEWS BY PEOPLE ON EITHER SIDE OF THE TABLE

notionpress.com

10
Bizarre
Interview Glitches – BIG 10

Blunders Made during Interviews by People on Either Side of the Table

Diptamoy Goswami

notionpress.com

Notion Press

Old No. 38, New No. 6

McNichols Road, Chetpet

Chennai - 600 031

First Published by Notion Press 2016

ISBN 978-93-5206-782-4

To all my dear dear colleagues and team mates
who have actually been my teachers
over the past three decades...

Contents

Reviews

Have always wondered if there could be a documented, detailed and candid feedback or evaluation of the interviewers, rather than the interviewee. DG has addressed this unusual demand in his novel book series the first of which is in your hands.

A heavily researched manual though put across very simply! The comic way of introduction is the author's unique style of sharing subtle messages which this opus is loaded with. BIG 10 is an Eye Opener and would suggest all to read it and read it well. Am sure you shall keep nodding through the depth of analysis and would be able to relate it even closer during your next interview situation.

Abhishek Gupta

An HR Freelance Professional – Chandigarh

A path breaking effort by the author on the art of conducting interviews, both for the candidates as well as the panelists. A 'must read' for all, irrespective of which side of the table one is for such events - adequately highlights the pitfalls to be avoided by both in order to bring in objectivity in the process. Case studies make the subject interesting and easy to comprehend. DG needs to be applauded for his effort.

Brig. Baldev Raj Bhatia

Noida

Filled with pearls of wisdom from extremely relatable interview conversations…this book is certainly one of its kind. Written in a thoroughly easy-read style, capturing the interactions in a role-play format is truly a masterstroke. Haven't read many (if not any) books that also focus on mistakes (glitches!) committed by the so-called powerful side of the table! Learning curve of the readers will get condensed due to a succinct, yet impactful diagnosis and the recommended solutions to committed errors. A must read for any professional, irrespective of the side of the table you are during interviews.

Rajiv Sachdeva

An L&D Practitioner – Gurgaon

BIG 10 is written in an interesting fashion, with compilation of real life case studies and their analysis. In-depth evaluation of interview questions and its impact on selection/rejection decision is explicitly highlighted. DG has accomplished this herculean task of painstakingly documenting each instance, which provides readers with insight into their behavior and its impact. BIG 10 on one hand provides valuable insights to both interviewee and interviewer, at the same time provides real life practical tips to enhance their effectiveness in making critical decisions for their life and organizations.

Dr. Maninder Singh Khalsa

An HRD Practitioner – Delhi

An Eye Opener for any Interviewer; absolutely amazing.

Mili Dutta

An HRD Practitioner – Ahmedabad

DG, as he is known to all, systematically and professionally implemented the pre-screening, Job Description, Critical to quality techniques in real time. In my interactions with him when he was HR Head & I was Heading two telecom circles, I realized, what I now see beautifully documented that the recruitment process is a two way scientific process where the candidate as well as each member on the recruitment panel need to carefully and scientifically prepare for the process. The book amply establishes the fact that the preparation on the part of the recruitment panel is as important as the preparation required by the candidate. The book justifies that the same is necessary if the recruitment process is to be successful and for the candidate to become a long term asset to the organization.

Rajender Sahani

Ex-Telecom Professional, Entrepreneur, Mumbai

A commendable effort by DG to document and present what has possibly never been done before. There is enough material available on Competency Based Interviewing but here in this book DG has presented the basic nuances in a very simple way which instantly appeals to the reader. The simple conversation style of presenting not only makes the subject engrossing but also suitable for any genre of reader. As DG rightly says, you never know when you may need these skills for interviewing your would be daughter-in-law or son-in-law…or even get interviewed by them. Keep yourself ready!!

Col. Shailesh

A practicing HR Consultant – Noida

In today's times of increasing competition where businesses are becoming more challenging and complex, getting right candidates for the job assumes lot of significance. Wrong or inappropriate choice of a candidate by an organization can lead to loss of opportunity consisting of; time, costs and productivity. While on the part of the candidate wrong choice of an organization or job profile can lead to dissatisfaction.

Diptamoy's work titled – '10 Bizarre Interview Glitches' is an effort in the right direction. He fills this gap by first highlighting importance of the Interview Process and then in subsequent chapters, giving live examples, how it happened vs. how it should have happened!

Author's candid approach is visible when he writes that, the word INTERVIEW sends a chill down the spine of almost all of us, irrespective of our background and experience. Such a frank approach to the issue gives confidence to the reader that, he is going to encounter something very interesting and useful.

The book covers interview process, as happened in real life, at length, highlighting minute details of the company background, position for which interview was conducted, background of the interviewers and the interviewee, the session of questions, their answers and special comments. In this way, reader feels being virtually part of the interview process. In between special comments by the author, on what went wrong and how should it have been done, gives deep insight to the reader.

I am sure, by going through the interview incidents and related analyses given in the book, both parties i.e. interviewer and interviewee, seating on each side of table will benefit and bring out what is most desirable – provide the organization with much needed productive employee and a meaningful and interesting career to the interviewee, thereby working out mutual Win – Win for both parties, leading to enrichment of both of them.

Vasant Kallola

Telecom Professional

Author of the book – *It's okay to fail, my son.*

Preface

(Must read before starting on the book)

Bizarre Interview Glitches is a collection of actual job interview excerpts with unusual meat for learning, both for a Candidate and for an Interviewer. All names and identifications are hidden or changed to respect the need for anonymity. However, the situations described are real, as experienced by the author, a practicing Human Resource Development professional for almost three decades, who has been on each of the interview panels narrated in this collection. The context in all these interviews is in India and for hiring for vacancies within India, usually for Indian companies. Having participated in tens of thousands of Interviews and Group Discussions, this is the first in the series of books that is being written, to share the experiences, for the benefit of all–yes ALL. All of us have to go through such sessions, throughout our lives. Be it a Job Interview, College Admission Interview, Project Scholarship Interview, Interview for limited seats for lodging and boarding in college Hostel, Internship Interviews, Interview with expert panel for upholding your thesis, an across the table dyadic between boss and subordinate for performance appraisals, would-be mother-in-law Interviewing her would-be daughter-in-law, a pampered daughter Interviewing her solo home dance tutor, a busy domestic maid (in a metro city) evaluating the housewife and her mother-in-law (her would-be new employers) or even the discussions during the first dating session between two people meeting for the first time, are all Interviews in one sense or the other–getting to know each other, a little better.

And that, is the most lucid and probably the best definition of an INTERVIEW, 'getting to know each other, a little better.'

Ironically, as simple as it may appear, the word INTERVIEW drives a chill down the spine for most of us. Even for a seasoned and thoroughbred professional, with chaste upbringing, the word interview is synonymous to EVALUATION and not just an 'exchange of views,' as it ought to be. The noble purpose of an interview is further damaged by the alter ego of the interviewers, who leave no stones unturned to convert the session into more of an 'interrogation.'

We are all privy to the aggressive media stance these days where certain widely acclaimed newsreaders take great pride in converting the live interviews of guests, invited by the channel itself, into public prosecution and typical court room trials. I wonder why the over burdened Indian Judiciary does not off-load its ocean of pending cases to such news channels. Speed of judgement along with total transparency can both be achieved; while there will never be dearth of such self-proclaimed judges, at least in India.

A little serious thought would actually reveal how arduously difficult a task it is to be able to conduct an interview in the correct spirit. Sharing my experience in this book, as I will, I have been surprised by the most unassuming panel members by their desire to step-up their 'ego' several levels up, to put themselves on a taller pedestal than the candidate. "After all," they think, "it is going to be MY decision that will get this guy the job." The moment such a difference of status is assumed; my job became tougher on the panels, invariably. On the one hand I would constantly have to invent different ways to neutralize the potential difference between the Interviewer and the Interviewee, at the same time ensure that the panel members' dignity and seniority is maintained. The candidate should be made to feel comfortable to be able to open up, yet s/he should not carry the impression that the panel members and the HR were on different planes. Having undergone so many training programmes on Interviewing Techniques and Etiquettes, along with the functional panel members, in almost all the organizations that I have served, I did observe one universal constant. Rather than understanding that the candidate is going to face so many of us, all unknown people, and therefore find it difficult to open-up in that short duration of 10–45 minutes, the universal understanding of Line Managers is that 'these days candidates are very smart and come with a lot of coaching on how to talk their way out in the interviews. Hence coming straight to the point is necessary–'cut the foreplay out.'

Surprisingly, the reason given above is also quite THE REASON why panellists should indulge in 'better familiarization' with the candidate so as to strike a chord with the unknown person, quickly, and maintain that friendliness throughout the session. What matters is the real thoughts and views of the candidate expressed candidly, rather than the 'politically correct answers,' which they may have come prepared with. The made up answers create a facade about the candidate which is, at best, a pseudo if not contradictory to what s/he really is going to be like, when s/he joins.

A job interview, therefore, has to be fair, where both parties can candidly discuss the job description, necessarily required attributes as per the role, proven skills and competencies being brought in by the candidate. Eventually, there has to be an 'exciting marriage' between the career progression being provided by the organisation and the candidates' true profile. Failing which, there will be a continued spiral of attrition, some of them even before the first few salaries have been drawn, many of them becoming negative brand ambassadors of the organisation, while damaging their own CV as well, as rolling stones or low-stability or low-on-compatibility candidates.

I have used the term 'exciting marriage' with a purpose beyond attrition. When the marriage between and employer and candidate is not exciting for whatever reasons, the seeds of dissatisfaction get sown, very early. If the candidate is actually smart and nimble footed, s/he will not stay for long and the organization will be losing a prospective contributor, too soon. It is a clear divorce from the candidates' side, which is becoming more and more commonplace these days. But in case the candidate carries certain inertia such as, spouse also working in same geography, children recently admitted to schools in the new city, parents undergoing treatment etc., the marriage starts to rot. A dissatisfied and disgruntled employee is now walking up to the office every morning.

Can s/he make the workplace better? Can s/he stretch and unburden the stresses of team mates? Can s/he be innovative or even take any initiatives? Likely NO. S/he is now calculating the payback period for all the costs of relocation and re-establishment that s/he has incurred by accepting this offer, which comes to…say 3 years. During these 3 years s/he would have further damaged her/his employability in the market. The organization then, has a 'classic furniture' to deal with, which is neither productive nor mobile. Painful decisions would follow depending upon the tenacity of the organization to carry such non-productive assets (or simply stated–liabilities). A little mistake at the time of interviewing can be so dangerous and with such ramifications. Both, the interviewer and the candidate are at fault for not having taken the interview session seriously and meaningfully, i.e. getting to know each other better, leading to a tragedy of errors.

Hence this compilation of blunders that we make in an Interview, both as candidates and as panellists, will come very handy to people sitting on either sides of the table. The current volume is limited to 10 such bizarre cases with their diagnostics and de-briefing on how they could have been handled better. For each of the interviews presented here, the blunder committed by the panel members or the candidate has been highlighted. Suggestions have also been given on what could have been done better, to avoid the glitch. However, these are not the only or the best solutions but merely suggestive. The idea is to take each interview session seriously, with certain pre-work amongst the panel members. It is not a session where the panel members need to impress each other about their ability to outwit the candidate, or to demonstrate to each other that 'look, even you did not know the answer to this.'

Panel members need to rise above all of these and assume those seats of judgement only if they can associate with the larger canvas of getting-in a candidate, who may often be even better than them, who can bring in new ways to approaching and solving issues rather than taking hackneyed steps, who will be respectful of calibre, not necessarily hierarchy and who will be collaborative because they understand the interdependence of team members to be able to reach a GOAL.

I would welcome your invaluable thoughts and comments, at reachout2dg@gmail.com.

Hope you find this book worth reading and more significantly, worth applying and practicing.

dg

Jan. 2016

Jaipur – India

Chapter Zero

Structure of this book

This issue of BIG 10 consists of 10 interview sessions for separate vacancies in different organizations.

These are real cases, as experienced by me, in my capacity as an HR representative on the panels, over the last 3 decades. All names and identification of candidates and panel members or even the specific organization that this case belongs to, has been carefully concealed. To this effect, at certain points, utmost precaution has been taken to edit the questions and their answers as spoken by the candidates, if they have lead to even an iota of disclosure of the identity of the concerned, in any way. All specific technical questions and specific industry data has been eliminated in the cases. The Job Profiles as also the Desired Candidate Profiles are (from various organizations) all in non-standardized formats and often insufficient in their detailing as well. What I have reproduced here is the gist of the profiles which just meet the purpose of this book. Any resemblance of the contents to specific styles of articulation or behaviour of any individual would be merely a coincidence, and I would not be responsible for the same.

The focus of this book is to share, with complete honesty, the behavioural aspects of an interview, not the functional/ technical part. In each of the 10 cases in this book, various facets of an interview from Take-off to Wrap up, have been covered. Glitches made at any of the stages, whether by the candidate or the panel member, has been highlighted, diagnosed and discussed. I have then suggested the remedial steps, both for the candidate and for the panel member, which could be applied to get a better experience and outcome in an interview. However, these may not be the only ways to overcome the problem.

I would be delighted to receive any comments/views/ suggestions on any aspect of this book, at reachout2dg@ gmail.com

Strengths and Weaknesses have we all, no one is born perfect,
We glorify our strengths and hide our weakness as if they are defects.
When we know we are all the same with little shades of differences
Wonder why we put up facades, doesn't the moon too have crevices?

Chapter One

Strengths and Weaknesses

Vacancy 1	:	National Head-Business Development (NHBD)
Designation	:	GM/AVP
Panel	:	Chief Marketing Officer (CMO), Chief Financial Officer (CFO), Head HR

ABC & Co. is a very large manmade fibre manufacturing group with their corporate office in one of India's state capital. They are hiring an NHBD for one of their premium product lines. The job description states that the candidate should be a Textile graduate and an MBA-Marketing from a reputed B-school. Must carry 12–15 years of Sales/Marketing/BD experience, should have operated in at least 4–5 prominent states of India. Strong analytical strength is a must with comfort in sourcing and churning large volumes of secondary data. Should have proven business acumen, strong market networking and be a confident articulator. Should understand stakeholder's points of view and convince them with data and logic on new ideas. Will report into the Chief Marketing Officer (CMO) and have a core team of 2 analysts at the Corporate Office. However, all State Marketing Heads will have a matrix reporting into the NHBD.

Excerpts from the Interview

Candidate, Ms. Swati Dhillon is in a business suit, sporting a boy cut very short hair style and spectacles. She steps inside the interview room, holding the door ajar, looking at the panel from the top of her spectacles, seeking permission to come in.

Head HR : Come in, come in Ms. Dhillon, we were just going through your papers.

Candidate : A very good evening to all of you gentlemen, I am Swati.

Head HR : I hope you didn't have difficulties locating our office, Swati?

Did you get a parking downstairs? Usually this is a rush hour…

Swati : Oh your office was there on Google maps, so no issues on that. But yes parking is certainly a menace here. I have my salon a few lanes down, but have always visited them on Sundays. Never realized, that on working days these lanes would be so crowded. Anyways, my son is there in the car and he will manage.

CMO : Are you sure your son will be able to manage? Else we could make some alternate arrangements…

Swati : Oh Sir, don't worry please, he is a 'pukka' Delhiite and in10th standard. By now he would have driven down to the Saket PVR and must have called a few friends of his, as well.

Head HR : Well then, let's get started by hearing from you about your upbringing, education, parents, likes and dislikes and maybe your family now…

CFO : Sorry to interrupt Mr. Goswami, I have some investors to meet in another 15 minutes, so if you don't mind, I have a few things to ask from Swati. May I…

Head HR: Sure sure Prakash, go right ahead…

CFO : Thanks dg. Yeah so Ms. Swati I want to know what are three of your greatest strengths and weakness.

Swati : Sure, but before I start, may I please know the names of you all gentlemen?

CFO : Well I am Prakash, Prakash Gupta, I am the CFO. And he is Mukund Parthsarthy our CMO, and that of-course is Mr. Goswami, the Head of HR, we all know him as DG.

Swati : Thank you Prakash.

Well my three strengths would be:

- I'd say I am very determined, can't give up easily, that is certainly my strength.
- I am a tough task master, people have problems with that, but as I said, I can't give-up easily.
- And then I am very detail oriented, love to get down to nuts and bolts, very quickly and almost invariably.

My weaknesses:

- I am a bit sticky about delivering right first time. Just can't glance through and move on, I have to know everything before I commit.
- Second, I find it difficult to digest unprofessional work or behaviour. Just can't take it, you see…
- And third, I can't stand apple polishing, for me a spade is a spade, period.

CFO : Well that's excellent and I like your clarity of thoughts.

Head HR : But Swati, the question was to spell out three strengths and three weaknesses. What we have from you is six strengths only…

Swati : How come? I didn't quite get that…

Head HR : Well you said you are sticky about delivering right first time. You can't digest unprofessional work or behaviour. You don't like apple polishing i.e. you can't stand flattery. Now just think and tell me aren't these all your strengths, garbed in beautiful words and being presented as weaknesses?

CMO : You are quite right, Mr. Goswami.

Swati : It's the way you look at it gentlemen. Day in and day out I come across colleagues who would submit their work, unchecked, full of errors, and just pack off from office for their evening activities. They would cut corners, compromise on processes and put up all kinds of unprofessional drama to suit their interests. They would ensure that they wish their bosses, the spouses and children of their bosses on all festivals and occasions. They would be complete yes men and blindly support even illogical view points of their superiors, just to flatter them. I can't do all of these and hence, I consider them as my weaknesses.

Head HR : Not liking something that ought not to be liked is not a weakness, Swati, it's a strength. Giving and taking bribe is a crime. Yet several people do it. If you can't, that's not a weakness. It's actually your strength.

Diagnosis

This is a classic glitch and a very common one. But there is more to the fallacy than just the question about strengths and weaknesses. Let's see them one by one.

1. *The candidate was on time, the interview was as per schedule and the NHBD was a senior position. Involvement of a senior representative from the Finance function was necessary if not critical. The not-so-committed presence of the CFO was not good for the selection process.*

2. *The introductory session is not a mere formality, it ensures that the take-off is smooth and a workable rapport has been established for the interview to move on effectively.*

3. *The candidate, in this case, is bold and confident to have been able to ask the identity of the people whom she is going to spend the next 30–45 minutes. As a rule, more than etiquettes, this must be done by any of the panel members at the start of the interview—usually by the HR representative. The introduction of the panel members can be very brief but it very subtly assures the candidate that we are not coming from a higher pedestal, that we wish to have a fair and healthy discussion with the candidate as equals and that s/he can be at ease with us too.*

4. *Now coming to the question of Strengths and Weaknesses, it is an absolutely irrelevant question for a seasoned candidate like this. Her answers and the discussion that followed are more than obvious that such a question thrown to anyone articulate enough is like a yorker. S/he will use it completely to her/his advantage, wasting everybody's time. Asking such a question to a school kid, at best, may be appropriate, thereby following it up with questions on how the child would like to leverage her strengths and what are her plans to correct her weaknesses.*

What could have been done to avoid such a situation?

1. *The CFO need not have been on the panel if investors were scheduled to come. The first lieutenant to the CFO could have been delegated to check the candidate's basic financial understanding. The CFO could have met the final candidate, later, if required, in another video call.*

2. *The introductory session is mandatory; you can't build your house and then start breaking the walls to insert the doors and windows.*

3. *Given such a shortage of time from the CFO, he should have asked a direct question on Finance to check the financial acumen of the candidate.*

4. *As for the strengths and weaknesses, the same should be derived through situation based questions such as "what aspect of your work excites you the most" or likewise "what aspect of your job do you find most boring or you would like it to be done by someone else and why"*

Say for instance, 'I am short tempered and tend to lose control on my language when I am really angry' or 'I tend to be too straight forward and miss out on the diplomacy that is so essential sometimes, to handle a delicate situation,' are genuine weaknesses, which many of us have, but very few will admit.

Therefore, if a certain job requires an ocean of patience, it would be better to ask the candidate to narrate a situation out of her/his actual work life where s/he had really strived hard to keep her/his cool, but finally exploded. Listen to the incident carefully and then question the candidate on the threshold point, where s/he lost patience. The example quoted by the candidate will give the panel two inputs. One, whether what has been described as a nerve testing incident is anywhere close to what s/he may likely face in the current assignment. Therefore the panel will get a fair idea of the grit required v/s what the candidate thinks, s/he has. Two, it will also supply inputs on the manner in which the situation was approached and any ingenuity that may be visible. At the least, the panel will get a fair picture, through this narration, whether the candidate is worthy of being groomed for the given vacancy, or not, on the given parameter.

…the interview continued…

CFO : (Takes the call on his cell) Yeah, I'm coming, I'm coming…Guys I'll have to go now, they've come. Well Swati, I will need to be excused, please. It is a pleasure meeting you. Carry on, carry on with the session, OK…all the best.

CMO : So tell me Swati, why did you choose Textile Engg. in the first place and why into Marketing thereafter.

Swati : Well I'd say things just fell in place. My mom is into export of ethnic Indian boutique wear to Holland and UK majorly and some parts of South America. My dad is an IFS officer and I have spent more time with him over video and phone chats, when I was in school. I grew up with my mum being my hero. Wanted to do exactly what she did and discovered that I need to understand fabric design and engineering so did B.Text. Then I needed to understand business operations, finance, marketing and management–hence MBA.

CMO : Interesting. So tell me Swati, two things that you've learnt from your mom, that they didn't teach you at B'School.

Swati : (Very spontaneously) That's easy, cooking and playing cards.

CMO : Ha ha…no I meant two business philosophies.

Swati : But of-course, I was on the lighter side too…Yeah, so my mom taught me how to choose a business partner, whether for supplying material or for selling your stuff, when every other commercial parameter is equal among the contenders. She taught me to choose the smaller vendor for whom our order value would be critical, the one for whom we matter. Get into an alliance with them as they will put all their heart and soul into the deal.

The other thing that I learnt from her was always to add a margin of safety in all our commitments, of any kind, to anybody. The delight that is created by surpassing any commitment to the receiver is far more rewarding than the margins of business itself.

And in both the above lessons, you are creating positive brand ambassadors for yourself, silently but certainly.

CMO : Very well said and pretty apt learnings I'd say, although the second one is the basis for six sigma; setting internal process control limits at half the band of the customers specification limits. Are you trained on Six Sigma, by the way?

Swati : Yes Sir, am a Green Belt holder and due for my Black Belt certification in about 2 months from now.

CMO : Cool Swati. So let me tell you about this role and how this position was conceived.

Then there is a series of questions and answers related to the specific hollow fibre product that was being introduced by the organization for the first time in India. The CMO discussed some broad strategies, and was trying to pick up her mind on evolving the nuances of the strategy, given the fact that two of our competitors were all set to launch their competing products as well, in the next 2–4 weeks. So it was this crucial 2–4 weeks that we had, to launch and take lead in the market. The discussions between Swati and the CMO went on for the next 15 minutes, while I was playing the role of the observer of the process as also the body language of Swati. She appeared to have captivated the CMO by her confident answers, involved discussions, aptly sprinkled with wit and humour. I was also studying her CV closely all this while and at an appropriate pause between the two, I chipped in:

Head HR : Swati, I observe that you have been in Delhi for the last 12 years and before that you were in Chandigarh where you did your masters' and the first job at the start of your career. Have you been exposed to any other part of the country, like Mumbai, down South or the East?

Swati : No Sir, very frankly I don't quite like travelling too. One of the reasons why I was keen for this position, it's based out of Delhi and your organization is also North India centric.

CMO : You must be mistaken Swati, I think the job profile clearly states that the position is for National Head of Business Development. In fact, I just discussed with you that the new product launch is in Bangalore, owing to its preference with Gen-Y particularly in the balanced weather conditions of that city. So have you travelled to the down South and do you have sufficient networking out there, Swati?

Swati : I'm afraid Sir, I have travelled to Bangalore couple of years back but, I don't have any contacts there. But don't we already have a set up at Bangalore?

Head HR : Yeah, we do have a small set up out there which is more into collections and local compliances. We need to quickly hire a few front-end and feet on street guys there, Swati, and I was about to ask you if you have some references for a quick on-boarding of some local guys from Karnataka.

CMO : That's right Swati, that would be among your first priority tasks, to bolster the Bangalore office along with our HR team here, and ready it for the launch.

Swati : That would mean I'd have to camp at Bangalore, immediately upon joining?

CMO : Yes Swati. Is there a problem?

Swati : No no no Sir. But…I seriously thought that I would not have to travel much in the next few months. My son is taking the 10th board also this year…and my husband's overseas posting gets over only in 8 months from now.

(Swati is beginning to feel the sand trickle out of her hands)

Head HR : Please have some water ma'am. Did you get my mail last week detailing the Job Profile and requesting you to visit our website for any queries about our organization?

Swati : Yes Sir, in fact we fixed up today's meeting in the same mail.

Head HR : Oh yes, of-course. So did you get a chance to go through the profile and our website?

Swati : (Visibly disturbed now, pulling out a kerchief from her handbag) Yes Sir, I glanced through the profile and your website was taking too long to open, so I skipped that.

Head HR : But we just heard you say that 'getting to the nuts and bolts of everything is your strength,' Swati?

Swati: (Abruptly, standing up and picking up her bag) I'll thank you gentlemen, for not rubbing it in any further. I have another appointment to attend, please, so may I now be excused…

CMO : Sure, thanks,(satirically) thanks for your precious time ma'am.

Diagnosis

There have been several interviews during my career span, where this Question of spelling out strengths and weaknesses has been sufficiently falsified. Candidates invariably tend to take it as a kite flying opportunity. But even I was surprised at the same mistake being made by such a seasoned candidate like Swati and hence chose to discuss it in this book. At the same time, our CFO should have been there to witness the shallowness of the answer and how easily it got caught. We did brief him, later and he was very kind to realize that the question about exploring ones' strengths and weaknesses needs to be handled very carefully, if not differently.

What could have been done to avoid this situation

Subject to availability of resources in the HR department, a pre-screening round is recommended. But more than that, it is strongly recommended to have the Job Description (JD) clearly state the Job Profile and the Candidate Profile, for all critical positions. The CTQs (critical to quality) should be derived from the Candidate Profile very clearly.

The given job profile may need very specific technical, physical and behavioural CTQs such as:

- *vision sensitivity to colours (i.e. test of colour blindness),*
- *knowledge of certain languages,*
- *sensitivity to differently abled children,*
- *need for excessive travelling, maybe 20–24 days a month,*
- *need to relocate or work on the fly,*
- *need to have one's own conveyance,*
- *working in shifts aligned to client's needs,*
- *specific knowledge of client's heritage or cultural parameters,*
- *need to have specific licence to carry arms, and so on…*

Candidates could be asked to specifically give their consent on such CTQs, before inviting them for the interviews.

The case of Swati's inertia to being mobile was particularly surprising as the field of Sales, Marketing, Business Development, Customer Care etc. are known to be travel oriented. This was clearly one of her weaknesses, which she chose not to divulge, even when asked. But her casual approach towards doing certain basic groundwork before presenting herself for an interview, was really unacceptable. Especially when she mentioned that she disliked unprofessional work from her team, she should have been walking her talk.

Last minute Changes of Specification is like redirecting an arrow,
Who cares whether it's still in grips or already left the bow.
Imagine the plight as you see the dead man falling on your toe
The arrow just killed the wrong man "Oh God – he was not my foe"

Chapter Two

Last Minute Changes

Vacancy 2	:	Lead-Treasury Finance (LTF)
Designation	:	DM/Manager
Panel	:	VP-Finance, Manager-Commercial, Head HR

DEF & Co. a pioneer in e-Commerce in India catering to the B2C segment, having country wide presence. The job description states that the candidate should be an M.Com. with specific training/certification in treasury management. MBA-Fin. could also be considered. 3–5 years of experience in the relevant field was essential. Good knowledge of MS Excel and handling large volumes of data and its' reconciliation would be part of routine work. Since the job may require stretched hours of working and frequent movement between banks, candidates living within 5 kms of the office and having their own conveyance would be better suited.

Excerpts from the Interview

Candidate, Mr. Praful Patel (MBA-Fin. with 2 years experience in Treasury Mgt.) is filling up the Application Form at the reception. The VP-Finance Mr. Kishan Agarwal has insisted to have the interview in his office on the 3rd floor. Head HR is there in Mr. Agarwal's office reminding the Manager Commercial Mr. Basant Paliwal on the 2nd floor, to come upstairs quickly, as the VP-Fin. has to leave for his daughter's annual function, in another half an hour. Meanwhile, a peon enters the office and hands over the Application Form of the candidate and informs that Mr. Patel is seated in the adjoining room. Mr. Agarwal gestures to the peon to get the candidate in and tells me "let's start, Basant will join…" Since Basant is the neutral panellist from a different function, I wanted him to be there so that we could discuss the profile and also Mr. Patel's credentials before starting, but, as usual, the interview was one among several things to be finished by the VP-Fin. in the next 20 minutes. He had already asked his driver to be ready and get his car into the porch.

Candidate Mr. Praful Patel, is dressed in simple office wear, carrying a bag pack and a mid range mobile phone, enters the room and walks up straight to the empty chair and drops his bag on the floor near the chair.

Head HR : Come in, come in Mr. Praful Patel, please take that seat.

Candidate : Thank you Sir. Good afternoon.

Head HR : I am DG taking care of the HR function here, and this is Mr. Kishan Agarwal, the Vice President–Finance.

So Praful you are basically from Ahmedabad, right? How come you are here, does Gujarat not have enough employment opportunities?

Praful : No sir, I am born and brought up in Chennai. My grandfathers had their business and settled down in Chennai. Two years back I shifted into this city for my current job. I do not know much about Gujarat sir.

VP-Fin. : (Chipping in abruptly) So Praful can you prepare a balance sheet?

Praful : (A bit surprised) A balance sheet? I mean yes I can, but it's been a long time, I'll need to see it a bit…

VP-Fin. : What do you mean, 'see it a bit'?

When did you finish your studies? Where from? What College?

Which year?

Praful : (Visibly upset and shifting in the chair) No sir, I mean I can do it. Currently I am taking care of the Treasury function, sir.

VP-Fin. : So are you telling me Mr. Patel, that since you are into the Treasury function, you are out of touch with making balance sheets?

Praful : (Looking at the Head HR)

Sir, I have come here for an interview for the Lead position in Treasury Management, that's why I said…

VP-Fin. : No no no Mr. Patel. That Lead position in Treasury is filled-up. I am now looking for a person in reconciliation. So do you remember trial balances and account reconciliation?

Head HR : Mr. Agarwal, what is this development? I seem to have missed out on something, is it?

Just then Mr. Basant Paliwal walks in with an ear to ear grin on his face. Completely ignoring that the interview is in progress and that the candidate is there in the chair, he starts off with Mr. Agarwal, in almost a single breath:

"Sir the matter is sorted, I've convinced Saurabh, I told him he is getting a chance to work with Agarwal Sir and that too in Treasury, he should just grab the opportunity. Finally he agreed Sir. I am taking Pushpinder as his replacement from Accounts. Have spoken to his Manager Sharmaji also, you know they don't get along very well. So he is also very happy and says this is good riddance for him. Sharmaji has agreed to release Pushpinder the moment he gets a replacement. So now we need a junior guy to take care of Accounts Reconciliation and maybe some small odd Bank related work, sometimes. I know somebody Sir, who can fit perfectly into the role. If you wish, I can call him tomorrow."

Basant then turned to me and said, "See Goswami sir, that's why I got late. But I've simplified your job, in fact you should be happy and take me into HR for solving your HR issues, isn't it?"

Head HR : (to the candidate) Mr. Patel could you please give us a moment. You may please sit in the adjacent room and I'll send in a coffee for you, if you don't mind.

Praful : That would not be required Sir. I know the way out, of this office. Thank you.

The next 60 minutes was a complete firework from me on to Mr. Basant Paliwal, initially, on his exemplary demonstration of immaturity. Without checking who the third person was in the chair, and without even anticipating the obvious that it must be the interview session in progress, Mr. Paliwal in his excitement to garner the blessings of VP-Fin., committed the blunder of sorts. He annoyed the candidate, and converted him into a strong negative ambassador of the Company. Basant did not score well in the eyes of the VP-Fin. too.

Mr. Agarwal however, tried to pacify me when I was giving it right, left and centre to Basant, and that is when I trained my guns on to Mr. Agarwal too. He was all across knowing the moves of chess being played between the Finance, Accounts and Commercial verticals, but did not bother to update HR. When the candidate was waiting in the adjoining room, just before the interview, Mr. Agarwal had the opportunity to brief me about the contemplated chain of movements. Instead he got the candidate in and changed the subject of interviewing, putting the candidate and the HR completely in the lurch.

Mr. Agarwal was made to realize his mistake, before he proceeded to attend his daughter's annual day function, 30 minutes behind schedule.

Diagnosis

Many of my HR practitioners reading this case would be associating similar situations that they would have also been through. To cut the long story short, it is the perceived non-specialized nature of the HR function that makes every department in an organization, try out the HR activities themselves, without understanding the science, nor realizing the consequence upon failure.

What could have been done to avoid this situation?

There is nothing wrong in creating an internal chain of transfers and role changes to fill-up vacancies, but that needs to be done in a proper manner. The Treasury Lead position could have been put-up in the Internal Job Posting (IJP) and thrown open for internal selection. The most suitable and deserving internal candidate could have been selected, fairly.

There could have been a suitable incentive for the section or vertical that would not take a replacement while releasing a team member chosen for another role through an IJP. That would have created a stretch in the roles of each of the remaining team members but with a larger pie of the sectional/departmental incentives, for each. Ultimately, that could have led to not having to hire, at all, from outside.

Certainly, this process would have taken a couple of months to be completed, but would have been far more transparent and professional. Employees would also have respected the organization for giving everybody a fair chance to make opportunity based career progressions or track changes as per their passion, competencies and merit.

Humour or Disrespect – the Slender Line, how many of us do bother.

"I am the interviewer and s/he's the candidate – I can say or do whatever."

But life is a drama where scenes change and so does the context and role

We must learn to feel others' pains and put ourselves in their sole.

Chapter Three

Humour or Disrespect

Vacancy 3	:	Vertical Head–Learning & Development
Designation	:	Sr. Manager/AGM
Panel	:	CSR Head, Head Operations, Head HR

GHI & Co. is a CSR Group for a very large service providing organization having country wide operations. The position, although headquartered at the Corporate Office in NCR, entails aggressive travelling for roll-out programmes across the length and breadth of the country. State L&D Leads (20 of them) would have matrix reporting to this position. At the Corporate Office the position is supported by a full-time Content Developer and an off-roll support for data compilation and co-ordination of logistics. Candidate needs to be well versed on web portal based L&D operations. Candidate should be an MBA-HR with proven background in Training and Development carrying 8–12 years of L&D experience, preferably in green field and/or start-up organizations. Should be a Certified Trainer on Behavioural Training programmes for middle and senior level employees. The position reports to the Head HR.

Excerpts from the Interview

Candidate, Mr. Saurabh Adhikari who has just entered the interview room carrying a leather bag in one hand and his cell phone in the other, had to wait for about 30 minutes as the panel members were assembling.

Head HR : Sorry to keep you waiting Mr. Adhikari, please make yourself comfortable.

Candidate : Thank you Sir, that's OK. And I am Saurabh.

Head HR : Well, yes of-course Saurabh, I am Diptamoy from HR and here are my Colleagues Mr. Rana, Heading the CSR and Mr. Agarwal, Heading the Operations.

Saurabh : Good afternoon to all of you, gentlemen.

Head HR : Well Saurabh, although we have been through your CV but it is always exciting to hear a little more, you know… so do tell us about your childhood, upbringing, your family, your likes and dislikes and maybe a little synopsis about your journey till now.

Saurabh : Sure Sir. I was born in Bhopal where my father was working in BHEL. I am the only child of my parents and when I joined Carmel Convent my mom also joined the school as a Teacher. Although a loner in the family I was fond of reading comics and story books from my early childhood and while everybody kept worrying that I may be feeling lonesome, my books never actually let me feel that way…

Head Ops : Well Saurabh can you come to your academics quickly? I wanted to know why you took to Management studies after your Graduation in Science? Did you not try for M.Sc. or MCA etc.?

Saurabh : Well Sir, my father did want me to get into Computer Science, but thanks to my Mom, she understood and let me do what I wanted…

Head Ops : You've not answered my question Saurabh; why did you not want to pursue technical studies?

Saurabh : Yes Sir yes sir, I was just coming to that. During my graduation I got steady with a classmate and we both wanted to be together, there on. Her parents would not send her out of Bhopal for her higher studies and so we both applied and got selected for MBA in the Faculty of Management Studies, University campus.

Head Ops : Oh come on Mr. Adhikari, this is a Corporate job Interview.

We are not discussing your love story here?

Head HR : (Quickly intervening) Well that's Ok…

CSR Head : Saurabh, I appreciate your candid and transparent reply. So what brought you to Human Resources Management for your specialization?

Head Ops : (Jumping in) Oh that's easy Mr. Rana, I can answer that.

His girlfriend was also specializing in HR.

Am I right Saurabh?

Saurabh : (with a pause and a firm straight look into Mr. Agarwal's eyes)

Sir, I would appreciate if I am not mocked around. I'm only being absolutely truthful here.

Yes, I took up HR because of my respect and regard for her choices. Despite all of this we could not get married, finally, because Hamida's parents vehemently opposed the inter caste alliance. Have not thought of marriage thereafter, as you can check in my CV, I have decided to remain a bachelor.

Head HR : (To the Head Ops)

Well Mr. Agarwal, I think this does not need to be stretched any further. I sincerely apologise for this, Saurabh.

Can we move on with the discussion please?

Diagnosis

This one is very simple and obvious of-course.

The Head Operations seemed to be in a hurry and tried to cut short the take-off discussions. He rubbed-in a point that happened to be a sensitive one for the candidate.

The initial few minutes of the interview are extremely important to build rapport with the candidate. To get into such a casual conflict at such an early stage of the discussions would have actually made the candidate to raise his guard. Mr. Agarwal became presumptuous and thought that he could pull a fast one with the candidate, without establishing that required rapport. Usually the candidate would either have kept quiet or blushed it away, uncomfortably. But Saurabh being a trained trainer and possibly good at public interfacing, did not get unnerved. Instead, he took the opportunity to set certain ground rules and made it clear that he would not like to be hit below the belt.

It is possible that if Mr. Agarwal had done a similar or even higher order prank, but at a later stage of the interview, by when sufficient rapport would have been established, even Saurabh would have possibly taken it in the stride and the outcome would have been different.

It so happened that the late arriving Head Operations was to proceed for his next meeting in about 15 minutes and was thus in a great hurry to meet the three candidates that were lined up for the post lunch session.

You will see how he further damages the discussions and the final outcome of the interview.

What could have been done to avoid such a situation

1. *The senior most person in a department need not necessarily be the best person to be on the panel. An organised person with abundance of patience and respect for the candidate, their time and their*

individuality, is a better choice to represent the organization or the function, in a panel.

2. *The art of interviewing does not come naturally to many people as they rise in hierarchy. Training is a must, starting from the top.*

With my three decades of practice of the art of interviewing, and more importantly, benefiting out of the styles followed by some of the most respectable and expert interviewers, my take on the subject is that usually, one of the following two approaches are followed by seasoned and adept interviewers:

A. **The Drawing Room approach** *with straight forward, direct and formal discussions in a very gentlemanly manner, checking references from the candidate on her/his views about various people commonly known between them.*

The entire session tends to be such, where both, the interviewer and the interviewee put their best foot forward. The green tea bag is held very delicately with three fingers while dipping it not more than two times. The ring finger is held out to ensure the diamonds are well noticed and the little finger is carefully curled at 12.5degrees away from the ring finger.

After the session is over and the candidate has moved out, a heavy factor of discounting would be applied by the suave interviewer, covertly in his mind, strictly out of her/his years of experience. The interviewer already has her/his views about the common known people and checks the adjectives used by the candidate, for them. S/he would then factor that if this is the candidate's best behaviour and such is her/his assessment about so-and-so, then the candidate's usual real self would be at best 60% of what s/he presented just now.

The above is a very complex process, as is obvious. But with adept application of one's intuitive sense and grey hair, the assessment does come out to be reasonably correct and acceptable and is used for very senior level hiring, where sufficient validation has already been done, for other basic parameters.

B. **The Living Room approach,** *the one where the interviewer tends to befriend the candidate, completely. The candidate is put at ease by being very casual and unpretentious (but very carefully, without being hypocritical too).*

The interviewer asks all kinds of questions but in a very positive manner. None of the replies given by the candidate is negated. The candidate is encouraged to be as carefree, as possible. The typical living room approach would need a bit of self disclosure as well. Hence, the interviewer does not mind sharing that even s/he got a back-paper in her/his second year at college due to her/his distraction towards her/his first love.

The candid answers from the candidate, in the completely stress-free ambience, let the evaluators have a peep into how the candidate is actually going to be in her/his normal work routine. Maximum elements of unnatural made-up behaviours are eliminated and the interviewer gets to know the candidate, a lot better.

Even the candidate feels very comfortable and light, during and after the session, as s/he gets a fair chance to cut the formalities and present her/his true self to the panel. The candidate walks out feeling, **"doesn't matter even if I don't get selected; but I really enjoyed the session."** *S/he is happy to be a positive brand ambassador for the organization, looks forward to join, if selected. S/he encourage her/his friends to apply for such an organization, for them to have that fulfilling experience too.*

…the interview continued…

Head Ops : No no no Saurabh, my intent was not to ridicule you at all.

You see, I like to be informal in my conversations, but please don't take that to heart.

Saurabh : (In a bit of an awkward situation) It's OK Sir.

Head HR : Yeah, so Saurabh, you do have some exposure to portal based L&D and e-Learning. Can you elaborate your experience on this a bit, for the benefit of all of us here?

Saurabh : Sure. When I joined the Alpha Beta Gama Group they were required to quickly roll out their 15 new centres in 15 states of India. Time was the biggest constraint as there were not enough trained manpower available for this new line of business, pan-India. We had to hire and train people for the basic processes and also the trouble-shooting support that they were required to handle, locally, due to the extremely low TAT that we were allowed by the customers, to restore any faults. E-learning was the only way out.

So while the Talent Acquisition team was busy hiring the new staff, I was able to tie-up with this e-Learning platform provider.

We then developed the 5 Basic modules and the additional 3 Trouble-shooting modules along with them. We gave them the content in ppts, with the supporting dialogues written for each slide. They converted them into their format with the voice-overs for the dialogues.

We insisted that for each module there has to be an evaluation process, 10 questions randomly selected out of a pre-fed question bank. Only on clearing one module successfully, one could move to the next. Unless all modules were successfully cleared, the certificate of training completion would not get printed.

We were able to complete the roll out successfully, with trained staff, in time, on the day of launch at all the 15 branches. I really enjoyed doing that project.

CSR Head : That's interesting. But tell me Saurabh how effective are these e-Learning modules as contrasted to the Instructor Based Trainings?

Saurabh : It depends upon the need and the subject matter of the course, Sir.

Let's say the subject matter is Situational Leadership or Group Discussion Skills or Negotiation Skills. These programs are best handled by an Instructor who can also create a mock session in the classroom to demonstrate the principles that s/he is imparting training on.

However, for programs on Standard Operating Processes, or Standing Rules/Code of Conduct, or Policies etc., the e-Learning works well.

Head HR : Well Saurabh, I see that you are a Trained Training Instructor. Do tell us what has been one of your most challenging session that you have faced as a Training Instructor.

Saurabh : (After a pause of about 10 seconds)

Okay…so this one happened about three years ago, when I was working with this NGO that was helping men and women going through turbulence in their marriages, some separated, some on the verge of, and helping them relook at the consequences and rethink. We had a fair turnaround ratio of about 20%, on such cases and felt good to have saved at least those many families from disintegrating.

On this occasion I was imparting a training session to 8 freshly recruited counsellors in our NGO. They were all meritorious post grads in Psychology, 2 boys and 6 girls from various parts of the country, selected after a decently exhaustive selection process. This incident happened on the last day of the four days module, that I was imparting.

As trainers, we are supposed to avoid, as far as possible, from becoming prescriptive or advisory. Looking at the age profile of these 8 trainees, I may have missed out on this aspect, somewhere, which these smart youngsters had taken note of.

Like a bolt from the blue, I was confronted by one of the girls in the class on a particular context by this question:

"But how can you be so sure about this Sir, you are not even married, let alone face such a situation of separation?"

For a moment I was shocked, next moment I felt like retorting not to mix personal life with professional. But I was able to control myself. I realised that Gen-Y is not like us and needs answers to all their queries. Try overpowering them using hierarchy and you've lost them, forever.

Head Ops : Oh no, not again!!

Mr. Saurabh why are you hell bent upon getting your fascinating personal affairs into this interview? Can you not take any other example which is above your failed inter-caste love affair? In fact, what I see over here, is that you have developed some kind of a complex within yourself and are probably going to live with that for the rest of your life. What do you say Mr. Rana?

CSR Head : (Bold and emphatically to the Head Ops.)

I COMPLETELY DISAGREE WITH YOU MR. AGARWAL!!

And if you don't have any more questions for Saurabh, please, you may want to leave us to finish the rest of the interview, if you don't mind?

Saurabh : (Already packed-up and standing)

Well thank you gentlemen.

I think I should be leaving now.

Diagnosis

A complete disrespect of basic human values and insensitivity towards others. Such set of people are just too mechanical and should be kept away from sensitive HR processes, whenever an alternative is available. Such people should be sent for the Basic and Advanced level courses on Human Processes, or courses on Introspection, Social Etiquettes etc.

What could have been done to avoid this situation?

If alternative is not available, such interviews should be outsourced to consultants who can understand the requirement as also the work culture of the organization and conduct the elaborate selection processes, themselves, preferably in the **Living Room approach**. *They can then send the finally shortlisted 1 or 2 candidates to the Senior Management to meet, in the* **Drawing Room approach**, *to take the final call.*

Pay me my Worth at least – or don't pay me a dime at all
It's a pity we spoke for so long and yet it's wasted time, but all
I am a silent worker I know not to blow my trumpet,
Don't exploit my situation that your offer I'd say "Dump it."

Chapter Four

Pay Me My Worth at Least

Vacancy 4	:	Supervisor-Electrical Maintenance
Designation	:	AM/DM
Panel	:	Head CMC, Project Manager, Production Manager, Head HR

JKL & Co. is a large highly automated manufacturing group with 6 plants across India, employing 3000 on-roll and 1000 off-roll employees. Annual group turnover exceeds 3000 crs. The group has recently committed itself to lean manufacturing and Japanese quality assurance and TQM programmes. This position will be responsible for all Electrical Maintenance-breakdown, scheduled and preventive, at the Central Maintenance Cell, reporting to the Head of CMC. The position calls for working in general shift primarily, but may also have prolonged shifts during breakdown or planned shut-down operations. An Electrical Engineering diploma holder from a reputed Polytechnic with 8–10 years of hands on experience, preferably in a highly automated production unit or assembly line, would be desirable. Knowledge of PLC programming and trouble-shooting would be of distinct advantage. Managing and supervising a team of 20 Operators (ITI/12th pass) would be an important part of the role, given the challenges of the 24 × 7 running of the plant.

Excerpts from the Interview

Candidate, Mr. Anil Verma, dressed in a dark brown and white check shirt with a black neck tie, blue jeans and a sports shoe has entered the interview room carrying a back pack in one hand and his helmet in the other. He had arrived 20 minutes before time, was given a form to fill up (by the receptionist) and asked to come back in 30 minutes. When he came back as told, his name was being called out, frantically by the receptionist and he was hurried up to the interview room escorted by a bell boy.

Project Mgr. : Oh! Where were you Anil babu, we all have been waiting for you.

Anil : I, I am sorry sir. I, I came here half an hour back and was given this form to fill up. I was just at the main gate, filling this form sir. I do not have a photograph right now, I'm sorry sir, I, I did not know that would be required.

(He forwards the form to the panel).

Project Mgr. : We already have all your papers here, sit, sit, take the chair, Anil babu, and next time never be late for an interview…

Head HR : Anil, you can have that glass of water, you seem to be sweating.

Anil : Yes sir, thank you sir. (gulps down the entire glass of water). It is very hot outside sir.

Project Mgr. : So what all PLCs (programmable logic controllers) have you worked with Anil?

Anil : Sir, Allen Bradley only.

Prodn. Mgr. : Can you make a ladder diagram for an Allen Bradley PLC?

Anil : Yes sir, I can try…

Head CMC : We need people who are well versed with PLC troubleshooting, not those who can try. If you are confident then say otherwise we move to the next question?

Anil : Sorry sir, I am out of touch, but I, I can learn, given a little bit of training…

Prodn. Mgr. : Anil, you have cleared 2 sections i.e. 8 papers of AMIE but you don't seem to be very confident with your subjects. How come?

Anil : No sir, I wanted to do AMIE but could not get time to study and did not clear any paper also. Hence, I have not mentioned it in my CV, sir.

Project Mgr. : What are you saying Anil. (showing him the papers) Your CV clearly says you have passed out 2 sections of AMIE in 2010 and 2012. Have you not checked your CV? Why have you given false information?

Anil : (In a state of shock, hands trembling, tries to look at the papers and find an answer)

I don't know sir, I am sorry sir, but I have 12 years of experience sir, and I badly need this job sir, please… sir, I don't know how this has happened sir…but I will work very hard sir

(he almost breaks down now)

Head HR : Are you Mr. Anil Verma?

Anil : Sharma, no sir, I am Anil Sharma.

But I have got a call letter for this interview sir…See sir, here, here it is…

(pulls out a paper from his jeans back pocket, trembling, and puts it on the table)

Diagnosis

This is again a simple and obvious error. The HR team usually hands over a list to the reception or even the gate security, at times. Although not a very good practice, there could be enough justifiable reasons for doing so. But that does not absolve the interview panel from having the introductory session, carefully. What needs to be done first, needs to be Done First.

Clearly the candidate's inability to answer a technical question would have been seen in a different light if he was not found to be pursuing higher studies. Maybe he would have been asked questions on what he has done in his 12 years of work ex. Most importantly, the candidate was clearly drained out and uncomfortable due to unfavourable hygiene conditions. A little familiarization session at the beginning could have settled him down and probably the mistaken identity could also have been discovered in a more congenial manner.

Although his correct papers were pulled out in a matter of minutes, but the candidate had already lost enough ground by way of his first impression (for no fault of his). This is a very unfair situation.

What could have been done to avoid such a situation?

1. *The HR should assess the workload of the front desk officer, before delegating this vital activity to them. Handling a vendor or a business partner is very different from handling a candidate, who is already in a state of anxiety.*

2. *The interview panel should definitely be more sensitive to the take-off session.*

3. *Any forms filled in one's own handwriting etc. are essential documents even from the legal stand point, wherein the candidate is clearly giving her/his consent to work for the given position. In case of any unfortunate incident, it is this handwritten form that establishes that the candidate had willingly consented to work under the given work conditions and has not been forced to accept the job.*

4. *All these need to be checked and ascertained during the first 1–2 minutes of the interview, carefully, and no interview panel should take this for granted.*

...the interview continued...

Head HR : Ok! So this is our mistake. Sorry gentlemen and sorry

Mr. Anil Sharma. Can I have that Application Form that you have filled up?

Anil : Yes sir, but I don't have my photograph sir, I am sorry sir.

Prodn. Mgr. : That's OK Sharmaji, relax, this was just a little mix up, actually we have one Anil Verma also as a candidate today and you see, your name is very common so all this confusion has happened. Never mind, just relax. Shall I order some tea for you?

Anil : No sir, thank you sir, I really got worried sir. Actually I am a very hard working and sincere person and have a lot of responsibilities on my shoulder sir. I am currently working with M/s XYZ Pvt. Ltd. for last 4 years. Now they are not doing very well sir, and are reducing their manpower sir. Every month 10–15 employees are being asked to leave sir.

Proj. Mgr. : Okay. So they have terminated you also? So when is your last day there? Or are you already free from there?

Anil : No no sir, I am still working there and neither have they asked me to go. But there is always that fear sir and I have a difficult family to support...

(Anil breaks down at this point...pulls out his handkerchief and covers his face)

Head HR : It's OK Anil. Please have some water. We can understand your situation, but breaking down in this manner will not help, you know that, don't you?

(Head HR leaves his chair and walks up to Anil, put a hand on his shoulders).

Anil : (Looking up to the Head HR and still in tears…) I am sorry sir, this was not my intent sir, I am just too scared about how I'll manage if I lose my job. I am really very sorry sir…

Head CMC : But why are you so scared Anil, you are qualified, you have good work experience, you are hard working and sincere, so why be scared? You can get a job anywhere?

Anil : I've been trying, since last 6 months sir, but…

I came here with great hopes sir, but, here also I am marked as late comer for no fault of mine sir and then my CV and AMIE, I will put my life into it sir, I promise, I swear by my children sir, I will do anything that you ask me to do sir. I will study and revise about PLCs and just give me one week sir, I will make the ladder diagram also and answer all your questions sir, please…

I can tell you what all I've done in my 12 years of work experience sir, I've learnt a lot. I have worked for 72 hours at a stretch sir, without a break, I can really work very very hard sir.

Head CMC : Just calm down Anil. OK, tell us what all you have done in the last 12 years?

In the next 30 minutes, Anil captured the rapt attention of each of the three technical panel members. He could not only answer every question thrown on him from all sides but once in flow, he just smashed the expectations of all the three. And I kept wondering why such a capable person did become so nervous and shaky in the beginning? By now Anil also seemed to be enjoying the volley of questions and his ability to answer each one of them, adeptly, was lifting his confidence, visibly. Intermittently, the panel asked him to draw and explain certain things on a sheet of paper and Anil seemed to have satiated them, all. I also noticed that in between somewhere, the discussion had drifted into Hindi and that made him even more confident.

Head CMC : Well, that was pretty good Anil. Over to HR now, we are through with our assessment, Mr. Goswami.

Head HR : Ok Anil, this is a Supervisory position and you will have about 20 Technicians and Operators reporting into you. So can you tell me if you have ever faced stiff resistance and refusal from your team and how have you handled it?

Anil : Yes sir, many times, but I have my way of convincing them.

Head HR : So tell us the most difficult situation that you have handled.

Anil : May I speak in Hindi sir?

(I gestured in affirmation and his eyes twinkled. Rest of the session went on in Hindi, though reproduced here in English)

This happened 2 years back in my current organization. For some unavoidable reasons the three weeks annual maintenance shut down got scheduled in such a manner that both Dussehra and Diwali got engulfed. The shutdown plan was ready by August end and as soon as it got declared, for all departments and functions to plan out their inventories and spares, there was murmuring within the workers that this was done purposefully, by the Management. Anybody who would protest would be given the pink slip.

My team of 15 was no exception, but as a Supervisor, I was asked to diffuse the situation.

I tried talking it out individually with each of my team members and although, singularly with me, they were appearing to be reconciled, the collective mood of the team would crawl back to square one, every evening. After watching this swing for 3–4 days I decided to address them collectively, one day. My Manager was also invited to attend the session, but I had requested him to be absolutely quiet, just an observer, like a fly on the wall. He had agreed.

And then I kept my talk very short and precise. I asked them how many of them had Police personnel in their relatives or friends circle. Some 4 out of the 15 raised their hands. I asked these 4 Operators to recall if any of these relatives or friends in Police have spent their Dussehra or Diwali or Holi or Independence day with their families, ever. Everybody got the point. So if our Policemen can sacrifice all their festivals, all their lives, for no additional compensation, year after year, why can't we sacrifice one year's festival for the sake of our factory, that gives us our bread?

There was complete silence for a few seconds and then someone clapped, another joined and in a jiffy everyone was standing and clapping for me, even my Manager.

Not only did my team, but all the employees who had to sacrifice their festival that year for the shut-down, did so with this example, and very willingly.

The entire shut-down went off, flawlessly. I felt very good about it sir.

Head HR : I feel like clapping for you too, Anil. That was brilliant. And how did you get this idea about the Policemen?

Prodn. Mgr. : Yeah, even I wanted to ask the same thing, how did you think about the Policemen, Anil?

Anil : My father was a Police Constable when he retired sir. All our lives we have celebrated all our festivals without him sir. He was our father but was never there for us, whenever we needed him the most, because he was a very sincere and hardworking policeman, always on duty, sir. When he retired he was invited to Delhi to receive a special medal, from the Director General of Police, for not taking a single days' leave in his entire career, sir. I am very proud of my father. He died 5 years back sir.

Head CMC : OK Anil, it was very good talking to you. So your current CTC is 6.5 lacs, right? But our budget is less, we will not be able to pay you that much.

Anil : (His face mellowed down, instantly) But sir…

Head CMC : See Anil, I have another important meeting to prepare for. So time is very precious for me. Our current Supervisor who has resigned, is at 4.5 lacs, isn't it Mr. Goswami?

Head HR : Sir, don't worry, I'll take care of this part. Actually we have one last candidate also who is waiting.

Head CMC : So let him go back. We are taking Anil na…!!

Head HR : No sir, that can't be done, he is waiting for last 2 hours and has come on our invitation. We will have to give him time Sir !

Head CMC : Oh you manage that Mr. Goswami and finish Anil at 5.0 lacs at max. I can't upset my CMC budget, after all.

So Anil, I hope you are OK with 5 lacs package? Now can you join on this Monday?

Head HR : Salary matters are to be done by HR, so please don't bother.

Anil : But sir, it will be very difficult for me to come down to 5 lacs. I have a lot of responsibilities sir.

Head CMC : Arey baba, you are anyway losing your job there, but you can't accept a lower salary here where you have your job secured?

Head HR : Now that's enough Sir. I don't think we have a practice of arm-twisting in this manner. The salary will be fixed as per the Pay Parity Matrix, and that's an HR job.

Thank you Anil, I'll get back to you.

(Anil walks out with a worried and perplexed look)

Head CMC : (Addressing the other 2 panel members, but basically telling me)

Gentlemen, just check out this last candidate whoever he is. Anil is OK but I am not taking him for more than 5 lacs. And I think our HR needs a course on negotiation skills. The kind of desperation that Anil is in, I could have brought him down to 4 lacs, I can bet that. The guy doesn't know PLCs, can't speak in English, is getting kicked out of his job, but our HR-Head wants to be his godfather. So how can we hire within our budget?

What followed was an unnecessary bitterness, with the matter escalated to the CEO. The Head CMC and Project Manager were on one side and I had the Production Manager backing me. Anil was invited again, a week later, and interviewed by the Chief Technical Officer and the CEO, together. They gave a special approval for hiring Anil at 7 lacs. per annum.

Diagnosis

Once again most of my readers from the HR fraternity will relate to the above situation very well.

The feeling of contentment that most interviewers derive, in discussing salary and haggling on it, must be ecstatic, I assume, because 7 out of 10 non-HR interview panellists enjoy doing it. While more and more organizations are now distinguishing this as a specialized job, to be done with utmost care and with a lot of homework done, by the HR only, it would still take another decade, if not more, for Indian companies to really get professional, out there. The Internal and External Pay Parity Matrix, its' creation, application and continuous updating is being done, very meticulously by many progressive organizations, today with the plethora of HR data and information that is available on the net.

But the real issue is not that. It is actually a cultural and a mind-set issue. Realization and acceptance of the fact that Salary is very personal and therefore a covert matter, is yet to dawn upon us. Although a crude example but I am tempted to state here that, while it may be perfectly acceptable to discuss the brand, design, texture, style or comfort of a shirt in public, one cannot do the same for ones undergarments. Such is the status of salary, but in reality, the more we insist and send across abstinence mailers, policies or communications on it's confidentiality the more is the urge for people to peep, explore and compare.

Yet for others, it is that sheer sense of superiority– "I will decide what to pay to him" that drives them to discuss salaries. Such people will use active voice in first person– "No no no, I can't pay you more than this…" putting themselves at par with the employer or the owners of the company.

However, the case of Mr. Anil Sharma, that is under reference, is bizarre.

All of the above fallacies are further topped-up with the desire to exploit his weak situation, by the Head CMC and the Project Manager. The departmental budgetary limits are important. But rather than taking-up the case for an exceptional approval themselves, the Head CMC and Project Manager thought they would be one-up in the eyes of the Senior Management by demonstrating such hard bargaining.

Or maybe their intent was to get Anil down on his knees, and then they would have got the Senior Managements' special approval. They would have then kept Anil under their thumb for the very special favour, for his lifetime in this company…

But, this is where the role of HR comes in, to ensure that such unfairness or exploitation of any nature, is not allowed to take place.

What could have been done to avoid this situation

1. *Prior to the start of the interview session, ground rules need to be set or revisited.*
2. *Any kind of arguments or strong differences of opinion must be avoided. In case of one, the same should be flagged for discussions later.*
3. *Exploitation of any kind should not be allowed.*
4. *Salary discussions must be done on a one-on-one basis.*
5. *All frequent panel members are required to undergo training on Interviewing Etiquettes.*
6. *Interviewing panels must remember that salary fixation is not an arbitrary job and therefore must be done by the HR only. Even the HR function should carefully do their homework w.r.t. any kind of serious aberrations or disparities that are being caused by offering a certain suggested package to a candidate. The CEO or the Head of the Organization should be apprised of the existing employees who may get affected by the offered package to the new candidate.*
7. *Salary negotiation is a very specialized job and should never be treated like buying potatoes or onions.*

The Rolling Stone gathers no Moss, so goes the age old saying,
It took time for roots to grow for every tree that was a sapling.
Not everything happens as per ones wishes, desires or vanity,
Accepting the crests and troughs of life is essential for stability.

Chapter Five

The Rolling Stone

Vacancy 5	:	Manager–HNI CS Escalations
Designation	:	Manager/ Sr. Manager
Panel	:	GM-Corp. Escalations, Circle Customer Services Head, Head HR

JKL & Co. is a pan-India consumer services group holding the second largest customer base across India, employing 7000 on-roll and 5000 off-roll employees. Annual group turnover exceeds 8000 crs. The group has recently committed itself to augmenting customer support and issue resolution, owing to the dip in the CSI survey for the third consecutive quarter. This position was created and sanctioned to be responsible for all High Net worth Individual (HNI) customer escalations at Delhi, one of the metro cities, which is also housing the Circle office for the state. Hence the position will be reporting directly to the Circle Leadership but will also have a matrix reporting to the Corporate Escalations Head. An Electronics and Communications Engineer having 6–8 years of experience in Customer Servicing, particularly HNI customers, will be required. Candidates having above qualification and more experience will be considered for Sr. Manager designation with suitable higher salary grade. The job involves high levels of stress due to fast escalations from the complainants. Sensitivity, spontaneity and patience to pacify HNI customer issues with calm and poised articulation and strong follow-up at the back end, were the prime requirements as personality traits.

Excerpts from the Interview

Candidate Ms. Usha Iyer is dressed in an elegant off-white cotton hand woven sari, with dark navy blue designed border, very thinly lined with gold strands, from Kolkata. Noticeably tall, her boldness quotient is visible in her below the navel sari tuck-line and the barely obligatory blouse without sleeves which she is sporting. Her goggles are up on her head, holding back her thick mane. The extra large 'bindi' on her forehead is unmistakably navy blue stick-on and not the usual maroon, in colour. A Jaipuri hand crafted peacock green and blue embroidered hand folio, held closely to her chest, was particularly augmenting the executive looks and all the members of the panel forgot, for a moment, that they had been looking at Ms. Iyer at the door for an uncomfortable number of seconds. Finally, she cleared her throat, smiled and said, "May I…"

Head HR : Well of-course, do come in, come in Ms. Usha.

I hope we didn't make you wait for long?

Usha : No no, its Ok, I was taken good care of, by your front desk gentle lady. Her son and my daughter turned out to be studying in the same section in school, so we had a lot of things to share and talk about, you see.

GM : How old is your daughter? Which class…?

Usha : Oh, she's about eleven; in class 6 in Jesus and Mary…

GM : You have an eleven year old child? Difficult to believe that!

Usha : That's the younger one actually. My son is in 10th

(The smile on her face was anything but blushing)

GM : Don't tell me Ms. Iyer, you certainly don't look your age, to be very honest and upfront.

Usha : Since I am used to hearing this, I do acknowledge that Thank you.

HR Head : So ma'am have you filled up the Application Form?

Usha : Oh yes, here it is. I did not have the photograph, so…

HR Head : That's ok. So ma'am would you like to tell us about your journey till now, briefly?

Usha : After my engineering from REC Kurukshetra I got placed with BPL and then to Escotel. I then moved to a start-up for about a year. I had to take breaks in between for both my kids, you see…Worked in a few start-ups in-between as well, until I moved into my current company about a year back for the Corporate profile that I was offered.

HR Head : But isn't that a rather quick change over that you are taking from your current organization? Everything OK?

Usha : Yes yes… better prospects, 5-day week… that's about it.

CS Head : But Usha, do you realise that in Customer Service and particularly HNI customers, one needs to develop a relationship with them. You need to get to know them well such that they also start recalling you. Don't you think longevity is necessary for this kind of a role?

Usha : Yes, I get the point sir, but I was keen about joining your group, since long. Had this vacancy come up earlier, I would have tried for it last year itself.

HR Head : That's not very convincing, Usha!

GM : So what is the structure of the CSD in your current set up? Whom do you report into?

Usha : Well sir, I report into Mr. DN Gupta, who is heading the CSD.

GM : So do you directly report into DNG?

Usha : Yes sir, but why do you ask sir?

GM : He has taught me in engineering college, 1st year, while he was doing his M.Tech.

CS Head : Oh really sir? You've never mentioned that before! Actually even I had a chance to work in his team when we were in Ether Communications. He is a very brilliant manager and his technical horizon is just too vast. He keeps reading so much and everyday he would share some new development or the other, from the world over, and we would listen to him very intently, because his information was always correct and unchallengeable.

GM : Yeah, we both entered industry together, I after my B.Tech, and DNG had by then completed M.Tech and also had teaching experience of about 3 years.

But my question to you Usha is that why do you want to leave DNG so soon? He is known to be transferring so much knowledge and skills to all his team members, that's what I keep hearing about him all the time and is also a very friendly kind of a boss. I mean, I am not influencing you because he is known to me, but generally people don't wish to leave him so soon, you know what I mean…

Usha : You're right, DNG will certainly be a great regret, if I take this change now. But then, I'll get a chance to work with you, probably, Sir?

For the next 15–20 minutes the discussion revolved around DNG between the CS Head, GM Escalations and Usha. Although I intervened a couple of times to break the discussion, but somehow the discussion would drift back to DNG-his magnanimity, the moving encyclopaedia that he was, his style of working et al…I had to attend to two important phone calls and therefore went out of the room twice. By this time the decision to hire Usha was already taken by the two panel members. Her joining date was also discussed and she had agreed to join on the ensuing Monday, i.e. 4 days after the date of interview. I was not at all convinced and resisted the hurried decision. I was told that she had all the qualities to fulfil the requirement, was very Highly Presentable, which would be an added advantage in handling disputes especially of high end customers and, could join quickly as well, which was one of our prime requirements. Besides, I was also told, emphatically, that Usha had already worked with DNG (as though that was also one of her prime qualifications).

Usha's remaining formalities were completed upon her joining which was just 4 days hence. On her date of joining she was escorted from the reception straight to the CSD Heads' office as there was an important con call that she needed to be a part of. Usha completed her joining formalities later in the evening, when she was escorted by a CSD team member to the Head HR's office at around 4:00 pm. Usha joined, worked with us for 4 months, became very careless with a prominent HNI and goofed up the matter completely. Just when things started to get serious about her role and her level of engagement with our organization, Usha managed to move over to another job, causing considerable damage to our HNI customers. Several other Circles managed to recover or stabilize on the falling CSI in the 4th quarter with the help of this new position in their respective Circles. But Delhi as a Metro city and Circle Headquarter, went down again on the Customer Service Index for the 4th quarter in a row.

Diagnosis

Usually we crib about empowerment, or the lack of it, and therefore decisions taken at higher levels not being in sync with ground realities etc. In this case, the Corporate had empowered the Circles to go ahead and hire this one senior position, directly at the Circles due to the criticality and urgency of this position. The fallacies in this case are very clearly the following:

1. *A very shallow apology of an interview conducted. The candidate made good use of her advantage on presentability. The candidate also played well on the weaknesses of the panel and manoeuvred the discussions well around the common known person DNG. Very smart candidate, very gullible panel.*

2. *Weaknesses of HR Head for coming under pressure of express hiring, thereby accepting compromises in selection process. Also, it is prohibitively unacceptable to have an HR representative on an interview panel, accepting other phone calls or any other kinds of interruptions. Even when the HR representative is not asking any questions, s/he has to be attentive and completely involved in the process, as a rule.*

3. *It is OK to be appreciative of the positive aspects of a candidate, genuinely, which also includes the appearance or presentability but never should the panel members cross the line into getting influenced or biased with such superficial aspects. Even if the CTQ for the role demands presentability as an important parameter, such as the TV News Readers, Flight Attendants or the Front Desk staff, the evaluation on other parameters such as diction, service orientation or ability to multi-task, patience, attentive listening and calm and poise need to be carefully assessed to be able to do the right selection for the role.*

4. *Getting carried away by the fame and glory of associates of the candidate is sheer immaturity of the panel. It is the candidate who is being assessed for fitment into the role, not her/his associates.*

5. *In the same breath, good interviewers take a note of great organisations that a candidate has worked for but do their own assessment about her/his fitment into the given role in their organisation and it's work culture. Thus, a Purchase Executive with all her/his experience working on SAP, MM & FICO modules may be a disastrous choice for working on an archaic excel based non-ERP environment, unless s/he is being hired for implementing and stabilizing the same ERP in the setup.*

6. *Last and not the least is the extremely quick joining date that the candidate agreed to. This is a very common temptation for the hiring organizations but this needs to be watched very closely. Even if a candidate is in her probation period in her current organization and is not bound by a 30, 60 or 90 days notice period, this kind of early exit could be on account of any of the following circumstances:*

   a. *S/he may have already been asked to leave, by her current employer.*

   b. *S/he may have landed herself into a hot spot and may be desperate to quit.*

   c. *S/he may be trying to renegotiate a salary hike with a new employer based on the hike that she got just a month back in her current employment.*

   And most significantly if s/he is capable of exploring and taking such a quick change (i.e. in 1–6 months), then what stops her from doing the same again, after being hired by you. Unless it is a short-term contractual or project-based association, such quick exits must be thoroughly examined.

What could have been done to avoid such a situation?

Apart from the obvious things, a reference check could have been done, when hiring on such an express mode. Now the reference checks or an antecedent check, as it is technically called, is a very dicey process. Most professional agencies, by far, follow the rule of not checking anything with the current organization where the candidate is working and rightly so. This is because if the current employer is spoken to, the essential confidentiality of the process is broken, jeopardizing the candidates' employment in her/his existing organization, while s/he has not yet been hired by the new organization. Checking about her/his professional and behavioural traits from previous companies beyond three years in history is usually of very little relevance, in the fast changing pace of organizational life. Hence most Reference Check agencies end up doing the usual, the routine verification of degrees and qualifications, a verification of dates of joining and exits of past 2–3 organizations, a quick check on the designations held and the salaries drawn. All of these are done very mechanically from the HR's exit desk of the various companies, who obviously refer to their databases and provide a very surface level verification.

However, putting aside a part of the negotiated CTC as a retention bonus, to be paid upon completion of the first year and then the second year, usually works well, in such cases.

But all of these make things complicated. They start having an impact upon the existing employees and their moral also. There is nothing better therefore, than to conduct the interviews exhaustively and in multiple sessions until you are completely convinced about your selection. Great places to work and exemplary organizations like Google quite rightly conduct their selection processes, for almost all their positions, over multiple rounds of web-interviews, by peers, superiors and cross-functional interviewers, from all over the world, spread over 4–6 months before they narrow down upon the right candidate.

Reference Check – Not that easy, nobody responds, they're all so busy,
Can't check from the current employer, they'll make her life so uneasy.
Who'd tell you the reality; why'd anybody spoil someone's future,
Interview well, have your own assessment, there's nothing really better.

Chapter Six

Reference Check – Not that easy

Vacancy 6	:	Support-Billing and Reconciliation
Designation	:	Sr. Officer/Asst. Mgr.
Panel	:	AGM-Billing, Finance Head, HR Head

MNO & Co. is one of the largest business houses of the country with wide diversity in its products and services. Although not the best pay master, MNO & Co. is able to attract good talent from the various competitors.

The billing function for the services that MNO & Co. delivers to its multifarious customers is yet to be migrated to a robust ERP. Until then the entire process is done on excel. After generating the bill for the last 30 days of services, the same is sent across to the respective customers for reconciliation and acceptance in the excel formats. This delays the billing process and the subsequent collections and thus is a critical function in the entire operations of the business and the working capital cycle. Sound accounting knowledge and a master hand on MS Excel were the only two CTQs, as per the job description.

There are 15 such positions in MNO & Co. 5 of them handling the 5 major customers and the remaining 10 handling the balance 35 accounts. The current vacancy is for one of the 5 major customer accounts and this is a clear poaching situation where the counterpart employee at the customer end has been specifically invited by the talent acquisition manager in the HR team, after ensuring that there is no agreement between MNO & Co. and the customer organization on no-poaching. However, the interview is sensitive and being held in a nearby hotel lobby, as desired by the candidate, who is known to several people in MNO & Co. and hence did not want to be noticed there, attending the interview.

Excerpts from the Interview

Candidate Mr. Devraj Patil had taken the day off from his office. He had requested the interview to be held in the morning hours so that he could attend the PTM of his little daughter at school, after getting free from us. Devraj had reached the Hotel 40 minutes before time, had filled up the Application Form and was waiting for us, practically, although, we were also in time as per schedule discussed. We walked up and sat at the same table Devraj had chosen to park himself, because it was in a corner with very minimal disturbance. Devraj only changed his position and preferred to sit with his back towards the lobby, possibly as a last measure to conceal his identity from anyone known who may accidentally drop by. We all respected his request and settled down necessary pleasantries, with coffee ordered.

Head HR : So may I have your Application Form with your photograph, Devraj? Have you filled it up completely?

Devraj : Yes sir, here it is.

AGM Billing : So we have already met so many times Devraj, but tell me why do you want to join MNO & Co.?

Devraj : Well sir, one is that the job is fully known to me, so I can start off right from day one. Second my travel time from here to my home will get reduced by almost 45 minutes. My daughter's school is also close and for my wife–her parents stay closer to this place, so she will also not get disturbed. Besides here I will get the AM designation too along with the perks and salary hike that go with it.

AGM Billing : But there you are working on an ERP environment whereas here it is purely excel based. So professionally will this be a movement in the right direction for you?

Devraj : Sir if you really ask anybody, the real challenge is in working with excel. In the ERP that we have, there is not much to do. Even if you are not sure about certain numbers, there is no way that you can go back and check. You have to only trust that the feeding from the units has been done correctly and move on. In excel there would be a lot of manual work, but at least we can check and correct the figures, if found wrong.

Finance Head : So how well versed are you Devraj on excel?

Devraj : I am not the ultimate, but I'd say I am good enough, Sir.

AGM Billing : Can you specify what is a good enough level in excel, Devraj? Can you do v-lookup, pivot tables, macros and programming in excel?

Devraj : Yes Sir. Have studied and done all of them. With a few weeks of practice I will be fully in command.

Finance Head : What is your reporting structure out there? Can you draw the structure on that sheet of paper please?

Devraj : Sure sir. (Takes a few minutes to put the structure on paper and writes the names of people in the structure as well, turns around the paper for all of us to see, and then starts explaining)

AGM Billing : OK ok so Mr. Rishabh Gandhi is still there? I thought he had resigned 3 months ago?

Devraj : Yes Sir, he had resigned, but later he was retained with a promotion and some 40% revision as well.

AGM Billing : We have worked together for 5 years in the same company in Ahmedabad before moving over to Mumbai. How is he to work with? You report to Rishabh, right?

Devraj : Yes Sir, he is my boss. He is Ok.

Finance Head : Just Ok?

Devraj : No no sir, I mean he is good, but a very hard taskmaster. He also gets furious if I take any leaves. I had a tough time to get today's leave granted from him.

He stays here as a forced bachelor and expects everyone in his team to come to office on weekends, when he does not go back home, to Ahmedabad.

AGM Billing : (To the Finance Head) Oh Sir, Rishabh was a workaholic there at Ahmedabad also. His wife used to come and crib at our house, so many times, Sir. He is a very cut and dry, strong administrator, Sir. Good friend of mine, but...

Finance Head : So that is one more reason why you would like to join us Devraj, isn't it? (smiles at Devraj)

Devraj : Quite right sir. Besides there is nothing much to learn out there. Everything is smooth and stabilized. I am there for the last 2 years and already work has become a bit monotonous, for me.

(AGM Billing receives a call on his cell and moves out, walks up to the lobby and out talking over the phone).

Head HR : So Devraj what I can see from your papers is that you have done your B.Com (pass course) through correspondence and a six months computer course from here in Mumbai. Any plans for further studies?

Devraj : Yes Sir, I've registered for MBA correspondence course but don't get the time at all to prepare for the exams, maybe after I get here, I would be able to complete that Sir.

Head HR : Well that's good, but why did you chose an MBA to pursue, why not an ICWA or a CS, or even CA?

Devraj : Sir, MBA is the easiest to do. Besides there were many of us who registered together, so I thought we could do some joint studies etc. That helps and a peer pressure also builds up when we see others progressing better than us, then we also pull up our socks.

Head HR : Absolutely correct. So have you not been able to take advantage of all that you just described–collective studies?

Devraj : Unfortunately not Sir. I needed some express money for treatment of by wife, recently, and took to stock trading. It went on for six months and meanwhile all others in my group had moved far ahead, for me to catch-up.

Finance Head : So Devraj how do you reconcile your monthly fuel consumption for all your units put together with the grid power availability? What norms of consumption do you assume and how do you factor for pilferage?

(I was waiting for such a decent relevant question to be asked for such a long time. Finally the interview moved into the right direction and a healthy discussion started off between the two. Just then AGM Billing returned. Almost at the same time Devraj's phone started ringing.)

Devraj : (Looks at his phone and mutes the call) I'm sorry sir, forgot to put it on silent.

Finance Head : That's OK so where were we?

(Devraj's phone vibrates again, and again, and again…)

Finance Head : Why don't you take that call, whoever is calling seems to be wanting to talk to you urgently.

Devraj : (In a little shaky voice, it's my boss, Rishabh sir calling)

Finance Head : Okay, so take the call and tell him that you are busy.

Devraj : Thank you so much Sir, I'll be back in a minute.

(Goes out)

AGM Billing : (To Finance Head) How is this guy, Sir?

Finance Head : Not too great, will need a lot of hand-holding, let me tell you.

AGM Billing : Then let's just drop him Sir, I'm not taking him.

Finance Head : No no I don't mean he's that bad either, but you will need to work along with him.

AGM Billing : I just spoke to Rishabh about him. He is more than excited to relieve him today. He is disgusted with his work. Says Devraj is always on the stock market, from the minute trading starts till the time it ends. His work is full of mistakes, he refuses to stretch even for a minute in the evening and what not…

Head HR : You just spoke to his current boss, is it? But that's not fair at all. You should not have done that!

AGM Billing : What are you saying DG sir, this guy is a big time bluffer. Good that I know his boss and I could just find this out!!

Head HR : But this is not done, it is unethical and absolutely prohibited. Without taking the candidate's permission you cannot talk to anybody in his current organization.

We have not yet decided whether we are hiring him or not, but he will get fired from his current employer.

That is why he is getting those calls from his boss, whom you think is a friend of yours?

AGM Billing : But how can we hire a guy who is known to be a bluffer?

Head HR : You need to find out that through the interview Pankaj, not call up his boss. Put yourself in his shoes and then apply your mind Pankaj. Why do you think we came to this Hotel for conducting the interview? Think…

Finance Head : DG is right, Pankaj, you should not have called Rishabh.

AGM Billing : But he is my friend Sir, family friend!!

Head HR : Then why does your friend have to call Devraj so frantically now, just after you have spoken to him?

Tell me Pankaj, tell me why?

You also said he is fed-up with Devraj, so this would have been good riddance for him and he could have hired another good replacement. Why not just let him go? Why is he creating so much fuss?

Finance Head : I agree with DG on this, we have made a big blunder.

(Devraj returns with a grim red face. He picks up a glass of water on the table and empties it without speaking a word.)

Finance Head : What happened Devraj, is everything OK?

Devraj : My boss Rishabh has got to know that I am in an interview with MNO & Co. He knows I am on leave but is asking me to report to office immediately. I don't know how he has got to know, but Rishabh sir is known to be very revengeful, he is going to fire me today itself.

I will have to leave right now sir, if I don't reach office in an hour, he is going to escalate the matter to our MD sir. (Devraj breaks down…)

Head HR : Never mind Devraj, we were anyways through with the interview. You should carry on right now, we will talk over phone, Okay.

Devraj picks up his bag and leaves as a very worried man.

Late in the evening Devraj called me and informed that he had been fired, his two months notice salary paid and dues settled. He had no office to go to from the next morning. He requested if he could join early.

I reported the entire matter to our CEO, who discussed the matter with the Finance Head and very gracefully consented to hire Devraj. A no-poach agreement was also initiated by the MD of our customer and our CEO had to sign it as they were among our top 5 major customers.

As for Pankaj, AGM Billing, he learnt a lesson of his lifetime and is still perplexed "How could Rishabh do such a dramatic thing?"

Diagnosis

This is again a syndrome that I have found people suffering from, their dependence upon the feedback of others, more than their own evaluation of the subject matter. Some people do it to avoid the efforts required in slicing dicing and deep diving to be able to take a call. They would become oblivion to the work environment or ground realities of the other organization or any special conditions prevailing in their setup that the candidate presents her/him self in the given manner. In this instance, Devraj's wife took to serious after effects in her health after she underwent an MTP soon after Devraj joined Rishabh's team. Devraj was severely stressed over a period of 14 months to bring about normalcy in their little nuclear setup. Sending his little daughter to school in time, her daily chores, tiffin and preparing lunch for his wife and lunchbox for himself was practically on Devraj's daily duties before getting ready to catch his 7:45am suburban train. On several occasions Devraj would get calls from his neighbours to come immediately as her wife needed hospitalization. Even otherwise, due to several complications Devraj had to take his wife to the doctor, almost twice a week, because of which he could never stretch in the evenings. This was not acceptable to Rishabh, as this went over for more than a year, quite understandable. Since the treatment was unfortunately beyond the group Mediclaim policy, Devraj had to have an alternate source for generation of funds. He could have resorted to unfair practices, which 8 out of 10 people do today, but as a conscientious person Devraj chose share trading, only to make two ends meet. With accumulated loans on his head from friends and relatives and the continuously rising cost of schooling for his daughter, Devraj had to take the share trading as seriously as his job. Rishabh never could nor even tried to understand Devraj and his genuine issues, which comes as a passing phase in everybody's lives. Such phases can become so casual if you have a humane boss and so treacherous, if it is with people like Rishabh.

Try putting a hand on the shoulders of that house-keeping boy, while you know you are going to leave your soiled boot marks on the freshly mopped floor, and just say 'good morning bhaiya,' before he wishes you, and see how your day goes by. Don't shout at the peon if your cup of tea is not as steaming hot as you like it to be. Instead tell him how much that tea means to you in starting your engine early in the day and see the difference. You won't need paper or plastic smiley sets to deck up your work area. There will be true smiling faces all around you, including your own self.

Ask that grey haired security guard with wrinkles of pain and anguish on his face but still smiling, how eagerly he is waiting for his daughter to complete her B.Tech because she has already been pick-up by Infosys during campus hiring at 20 times the starting salary than what he gets home including his army pension. Give him a chance to feel proud and wipe his tears of joy as he narrates this to you. Just try it, it costs nothing but reassures you that you can consider skipping your annual cardiac check-up because your heart is working very well and is right there, where it ought to be.

What could have been done to avoid such a situation?

Very obvious, allow the HR people to do their job, while you do yours. Members on the interview panel are required to do a now and here basis assessment of the candidate, check thoroughly on whether the competencies and skills required to shoulder the current role's CTQs are well in place in the candidate. The length, breadth, depth and dimensions of skill tests, group task evaluation and layers of interviews have to be so strong that nothing much is left on reference checks. Reference checks are evaluations of others whose quality standards could be different from ours.

As a rule, unless the candidate gives consent, no one in the current organization should be spoken to; the likes of Rishabh are sitting in every department, every organization, every family.

In case the candidate has worked only in one organization or has worked in other organizations too long ago (usually more than 3 years ago), the HR function will have to find out through their networking or from their own existing employees' data base, if any other employee has joined from the same or related companies. HR may then approach the said person educating her/him completely about the sensitivity of such information and then collect feedback about the candidate under subject. But the whole process needs time and patience. If none is available then it is better to avoid and rely completely on one's own evaluation of the candidate.

Aggression or Gender Bias, wonder why we discriminate,
We still expect our female counterparts to be coy and sedate.
Why should performance and calibre not be the only measure?
When a lady overtakes today why do men get displeasure?

Chapter Seven

Aggression or Gender Bias

Vacancy 7	:	Management Trainee
Designation	:	MT (Manager-on confirmation in 6 months)
Panel	:	Head B2C, CFO, GM-Strategy, GM-Operations, Head HR

PQR & Co. is a B2B manufacturing group but has now planned to become B2C for certain lines of products, to begin with. It has created a name and goodwill in the industrial circles as one of the technologically most sound and state-of-the-art manufacturer and knows the nuances of the game very well, w.r.t. Engineering excellence. However, stepping into the B2C arena is a very different ball game. Creating brand awareness and recall, mass media appearance, add campaigns, sales and distribution channels and their management, pricing strategies and product launches and the hype management, influencing consumer perception, customer satisfaction indices, promotions and Customer Relationship Management et all... are new challenges for the group. A seasoned maverick has already been hired over a 3 hour over-the-flight interview (at 40,000 feet asl) by the CEO, to Head the new B2C SBU. The new Head B2C wishes to hire some extremely smart, out of box thinkers with fire in their belly. 7 CVs shortlisted for the position are all MBAs due to pass out from top B-schools in another semester, with engineering backgrounds from some of the best engineering colleges in India. All the candidates have been invited to the corporate office of PQR & Co. for an off-campus hiring. They have been observed by each of the panel members during two group discussion sessions which lasted for a full hour.

Excerpts from the Interview

The candidate Ms. Shabnam Bano, has appeared to be a fire brand, never-settling, fiercely articulate young lady with a 64 GB RAM and 8 TB Memory, to put it in today's IT parlance. The amount of data about the Indian economy and the global benchmarks that she was able to blurt during the first GD topic "Can we do without foreign technology" was breath-taking. She actually left the other 6 participants scratching their heads and reaching out for their glasses of water. In the subsequent GD on "Which is a better options in today's scenario–a joint or a nuclear family" Shabnam hardly gave any room for the others to speak. The observers had noticed that every point that she made in support of a nuclear family in today's jet paced, DISC or even DINK families (Dual Income Single Child and Dual Income No Kid), was valid. Specific and ample data again, both for families in the Metro and semi-Metro cities v/s families from B and C class cities was tabled by Shabnam. As a matter of fact, she had darted into the second GD so gallantly, taking minor support from the only other female participant in the group, that she almost made the discussion sound like a ladies topic and literally kept the other 5 male folks, in the group but on the periphery. In the last one minute of the GD, Shabnam's aggressive attempt to forge a consensus was thwarted by two male candidates who had initially supported the nuclear family. They were clearly annoyed by such fierce monopoly of Shabnam and changed their stance at the concluding moment. The GD had to be ended, undecided, but the observers (who were now the interview panel members) had enough inputs about Shabnam, her super IQ and aggressiveness.

HR Head : Come in Ms. Shabnam Bano, please be seated.

Shabnam : Thank you sir. Good afternoon Gentlemen.

Head B2C : At the outset I must admit Shabnam, I am impressed by the amount of reading that you do and more than that, your penchant for data and numbers. How do you remember so much statistics, at this age?

Shabnam : (Pushing her spectacles up on her nose) Thank you Sir. I have been complimented on this by my professors too.

How do I do it…well I guess when I am not sleeping, I am either reading or debating with my Mom or Dad on various national and global issues or studying for my curricula. So that gives me enough reason to keep referring to the data and numbers that I pick up from books and magazines. I guess my frequent reference to the data makes me remember them.

Head B2C : So who all do you have in your family?

Shabnam : We are also a nuclear setup. (smiles only)

I am the only child and my Mom and Dad. Occasionally my grandmother drops by, stays with us for a couple of months and then moves on to other relatives.'

Head HR : And what do your parents do?

Shabnam : They are both Professors at Delhi University, North Campus.

Head B2C : Whom have you taken on, your Mom or your Dad?

Shabnam : Both, I guess. I picked-up my reading habits from my Mom, and debates and discussions from my Dad.

GM Strat. : OK Shabnam before we get into other things, I am keen to know about your experience in the GD that you just participated in, this morning. What is your take on it?

Shabnam : It was good Sir. I mean we have lost more than 50 years establishing and consolidating ourselves as an independent nation. The world has moved much ahead, meanwhile. So rather than re-inventing the wheel it is better we buy the technology from wherever it is available and then build on it to surge ahead as a Technological front runner. I agree that the technology that will be made available to us by any nation would be their outdated ones and we will have to pay through our nose, to even get that. But in a politically and socially unstable country like ours, we have no choice but to take up whatever we can get and afford.

CFO : What do you mean by political and social instability?

Shabnam : Sir, if you permit I'd like to answer that with an example of Japan. In 1945, Japan was subjected to two atomic bombs with more than 3 lac deaths and the largest destruction of property and infrastructure as an outcome of a war known to mankind. That was around the same time as we got our independence, right, 1947. The damages faced by Japan were many folds larger than the damages that we faced in getting our independence and the partition thereafter.

Look at Japan today, w.r.t. technological advancement and look at India.

CFO : Point taken.

GM Ops. : But madam, what happened in the second GD topic. You seemed to have dominated it completely?

Shabnam : Is that so? I thought everybody did make their point for about 2 minutes each, sequentially, in the beginning.

GM Ops. : But madam after that you never let anyone else speak. You projected the topic as one which only the girls could take a call on?

Shabnam : Well that's a serious observation that you are making Sir. Let me clarify, that was not the least of my intent.

(Shabnam pushes her spectacles back and up on her nose)

GM Ops. : Madam, did you notice… (Shabnam interrupts…)

Shabnam : Sir I am Shabnam, you can call me by my name.

GM Ops. : OK Shabnam, did you notice that two of your male participants changed their views at the last minute?

Shabnam : Yes sir, even I found it a bit odd, but if I was given another 2–3 minutes, I would have convinced them.

GM Ops. : But why do you think they would have changed their views?

Shabnam : They may have been fence sitters initially when they gave their opinion and firmed-up their minds later. It happens…

GM Ops. : Or was it that they were not happy with your aggression and the way you converted it into a subject matter of ladies' expertise?

Shabnam : (With a stern voice) I have already clarified that that was not the intent at all. But now that you've mentioned it yet again Sir, let me give you some facts about our back stage discussions, after the GD was over and while we have waited for the interviews to start. Each one of the 5 male folks in our group has congratulated me for the GD participation. We are all from different colleges and therefore we are meeting each other for the first time. All the participants are brilliant and must be so to have come up to this stage of your selection process. If there was any element of the female chauvinism that you are hinting me for, they would not have bothered to come and talk to me or befriend me.

GM Ops. : That is only out of courtesy that they have spoken to you. I know exactly what they felt about your aggressiveness…

(HR Head interrupts)

HR Head : Well that's OK Mr. Mittal. I think…

(Shabnam interrupts)

Shabnam : I am sorry Sir, but I think it is Mr. Mittal who is himself not happy about my aggression. So I want to ask you Mr. Mittal if it had been any of the male participants in the group doing the same that I did, would you have questioned him as much about his aggression?

Head B2C : That's enough Shabnam. You did defend yourself very well. But now you are going overboard. Shall we carry on with the interview now?

Shabnam : I know I have screwed up my chances of getting selected, out here. But just tell me gentlemen, I am fond of reading, I am fond of collecting data, I am fond of debates and discussions, I am able to recall data whenever it is required and therefore I tend to be a little more confident than others, in group discussions and debates. But that should not be misconstrued as aggression?

And even if it is aggression, it is not negative aggression that the corporate world should be worried about?

GM Ops. : Are we interviewing you or are you interviewing us?

Shabnam : There are 6 more candidates waiting to be interviewed Sir. I think I am in the wrong place and need to be excused.

(She gets up and walks out of the room).

After interviewing all the candidates, the Head B2C, who had to take the final call, declared Shabnam as selected, along with 2 others in the group of 7. He was particularly impressed about her attitude and positive aggression, both of which were required in the challenging role that was at hand.

Diagnosis

Yes Shabnam was fiercely bold. One in a million who have the audacity to retort in an interview the way she did. But she was also very different. At a peer group level, despite her aggressiveness she had managed to befriend and gel well with the others.

Panel members have a tough task, particularly when they meet the Gen-Y. Turning around and asking a reverse question to any seniors is unthinkable for the Gen-X panel member. Not so uncommon for the bold and straight forward youngsters. After reading this interview most people would say that Shabnam is cut out for the Indian Administrative Services, qualified, well read, gutsy and straight forward. And that's exactly what the Head B2C was looking for.

Most of the panel members felt that Shabnam had bull dozed the GD to her advantage. But the GM-Ops. had possibly taken it a little too seriously. He was a man of the old school, where girls had to be shy and soft-spoken if not lip sealed. Working in industry Mr. Mittal could graduate upto a point where he could tolerate a working girl to be able to speak up when asked. But speak up as Shabnam did was far beyond the acceptable threshold of Mr. Mittal.

We have innumerable Mr. Mittals among us who only pretend to be having a modern outlook. They pretend to have embraced the gender equality very well, but heart-of-hearts they still are the traditional typical domineering MALE. Not all of these pseudo modern people will behave in the same manner, many may just become silent, walk away or some may even be overwhelmed and blurt out "My my…" and promise deep within, "I am not going to allow my daughter to grow up like that"

What could have been done to avoid such a situation?

1. *Training the panel members is of paramount importance.*
2. *The interview panel for such Gen-Y candidates should have more of the younger panel members who identify themselves well with the young minds. Even the candidates feel more comfortable with such panellists.*
3. *Panel members need to exhibit very high standards of maturity. Particularly in such cases where the candidate is hovering over her/his threshold of patience. Unless the JD so demands that a stress situation be created to test the candidates' resilience index, it is the panel member's duty to be alert when to draw that line of safety.*

Cases documented in this book may appear to be exceptional in nature. Ones that usually do not happen in day to day routine. But it is such unusual cases that also have the potential to challenge the unstated norms.

Panel members are usually senior employees of organizations who already have enough accomplishments to back them up. Nobody questions their follies in an interview sessions. All misgivings are credited to the candidate and her/his immaturity. Very few would realize that as panel members there is an ocean of patience required to be demonstrated. As panel members, they have to be much above their own beliefs and preferences.

As panel members they have to be prepared to meet candidates who have much higher potential than them, sometime – candidates who are going to define new horizons of performance and achievements.

Transparency Always Helps – truthfulness' a timeless virtue,

And yet we try to distort, and dress-up what is untrue.

As one thing leads to the other, one cover-up needs another

Until it gets all so complex – the original, one doesn't remember.

Chapter Eight

Transparency Always Helps

Vacancy 8	:	Lead-Information Security
Designation	:	Manager/ Sr. Manager
Panel	:	CIO, External Expert-Consultant, CFO, Head HR

STU & Co. is a very large infrastructure and service provider organization which had proclaimed its' penchant for quality, very early, by getting an appropriate ISO certification. By the nature of its' business STU & Co. has a very large asset base that is scattered across each of its' functional cells through the length and breadth of the country. The organization is also very advanced in terms of use and application of IT. Not only is the dynamic record of its large asset base needs to be constantly updated, it has also provided access to its major customers on to its own cloud based operations package. Connecting the vendors is also on the cards. All this needs to be handled very professionally with abundant firewalls and information security gateways, such that critical business information is prevented from any kind of unauthorized access. B.Tech in Information Technology/MCA, with suitable information security certifications is a must. At least 6–8 years of similar field experience is desired. Self learner and passion for upgrading oneself would be necessary. Organization will support for all trainings and upgrade certifications. Driving the new IT Security Policy across the organization and ensuring 'Zero Leak' is a prime KRA.

Excerpts from the Interview

Candidate, Mr. Nitin Manjhrekar is late by 30 minutes, stuck in morning traffic. Although he had informed the Talent Acquisition lady, she herself got late and had requested the Front Desk lady to take care. By the time Nitin entered the interview room, the panel had finished their first round of tea/coffee and had moved on to study the CV of the second candidate, Preeti Patel who was scheduled for 10:00 am.

Head HR : Come in, come in Nitin, you are late by half an hour.

Nitin : I am really sorry sir, I got stuck in a very bad traffic jam.

CFO : Correct Nitin but we all face the same conditions this morning, isn't it?

Nitin : As I said Sir, I am extremely sorry, I should have started earlier.

Consultant : So Nitin do you drive yourself or use public transport?

Nitin : Yes Sir, I drive an SUV, purchased it second hand, recently.

Head HR : So shall we start? Or would you like to have a cup of tea or coffee Nitin?

Nitin : No no sir, we can start, I have an updated version of my CV, have sent it to you, Mr. Goswami, just an hour back,. Shall I open it on my tab for everyone to see?

Head HR : No no, when you are here with us we would rather hear it straight from you. So do tell us about your early childhood, parents, upbringing, likes and dislikes, and why you took up IT as a career?

Nitin : I did my 10th ICSE from Christ the King High School, Jhansi, and 12th from Maharashtra State board from Pune. My interest was always in cracking passwords, in fact I had the passwords of all the students of my class, all my Teachers' and even my Principal Sir's. During my graduation I was able to get relaxation in ragging as I could help my seniors hack into our Professor's laptops and all the college computers. I used to become very popular with students of all faculties, even from other colleges, because of this.

CFO : Well that's interesting. What about your parents, did they know about this and what did they have to say?

Nitin : My father knew a little about it and was worried that I should not misuse this skill. He once even told me that in his days people who could open locks were invariably suspected to be thieves. My mother is a home maker and was only happy that I did not get ragged and beaten up at college. She was happy that I had lots of friends and would make it a point to serve tea and snacks to all my friends, whenever they'd drop by.

Due to my popularity at College, even my only younger brother got a lot of advantage all through, though he has completely different interests. He took up Geology and has just got placed in GSI, Dehradun, after his masters.

Head HR : As I am listening to you Nitin, I have a feeling, have we met earlier?

Nitin : I don't think Sir, I mean, I do not recall having seen you earlier.

(However, there is a distinct change in his tone and body language now… He appears to have become a little conscious and starts avoiding eye contact with me. I picked-up his CV and started reading it carefully)

CIO : So that explains your choice of taking up a career in IT. But why did you not take the traditional course of a B.Tech in Computer Science etc. You rather went for BA (Mathematics) and then MCA?

Nitin : Sir, I was certain that I did not want to do engineering. Civil services was my dream. So I did my BA with Mathematics, which was my pet subject, and started preparing for the Civil Services, parallely.

CFO : Interesting Nitin. So did you get through the Civil Services?

Nitin : Sir, I got through the prelims and mains in my first attempt, but could not clear the final Interviews. I took a second attempt but again with the same outcome. It was then that I decided to do MCA.

(Nitin is looking at me from the corner of his eye and is visibly worried that I am still reading his CV, very intently.)

Head HR : (Meanwhile I have recalled the context in which I had seen Nitin's photograph in a newspaper, few years back)

How many attempts did you take at the Civil Services exams, Nitin?

Nitin : Sir, two only…

Head HR : Which were the years?

Nitin : Sir, I will need to recall, let me see…

(opens his tab, flips through the screens, visibly nervous, there is silence in the room…)

Head HR : You said Civil Services was your dream, but you don't recall the years that you attempted…?

Nitin : (In a clearly shaken voice…) It's just slipping off my memory…I need to be excused, I'll have some water and come back please…

Head HR : Sure. Water is here. (passing over the filled glass of water towards Nitin) Is there anything you would like us to know Mr. Manjhrekar?

Nitin : Sir, it was 1991 and 1992 that I took the Civil Services exams…

Head HR : But you did your 12th in 1985. You would have done your graduation by 1988, right. But then what did you do between '88 and '91 Mr. Manjhrekar? You said you were preparing for the IAS, parallely, right?

Nitin : No no Sir, I graduated in 1990. I did my graduation privately, through IGNOU.

CFO : Cough it out Nitin, what really is the matter?

Nitin : Sir, sir I am sorry, I have to leave right now, I suddenly remembered a very urgent work I need to attend to…

(picks up his bag and rushes out of the room)

Diagnosis

This is one of my classic experiences where the significance of the take-off session in an interview is aptly demonstrated.

Mark the difference, here is an organization which has undergone Interviewing Techniques' training. All the members on the panel and fortunately even the external Consultant are in sync with the others and do not hurry up with the introductory session, despite the fact that the panel has been waiting for this first candidate and lost 30 minutes of their crucial morning hours.

With a little effort, after the candidate exited in the peculiar manner that it was, I was able to recall and inform the panel that Nitin Manjhrekar was charged and proven guilty of leaking out the University examination papers, in 1986. He was rusticated from the University and debarred from taking admission in any other University for 3 years. Most newspapers carried his photograph and the story. Finally he completed his BA through IGNOU in 88–90. He did get enough time to prepare for Civil Services and with his intrinsic intelligence, cleared the same twice, but could not withstand the interviews.

In case the familiarization session was cut short, the discussion would have started straight away from the quality of experience, accomplishments etc. It is important to note here that most organizations would not subscribe to the view "once a convict, always a convict," as was the case of STU & Co. also. As a combined view of the panel, if Nitin had presented himself transparently, his candidature stood a good chance to merit consideration. Because, all said and done, Nitin Manjhrekar had been working in good organizations over the past 6 years and had certainly moved on in his life after the 1986 incident. His attempt to cover up this crime of his life through blatant lies, is what came under severe objection, as doubtful integrity.

The entire company's confidential information would have been in his hands, which he, in his role of Lead-Information Security, needed to actually protect through an error free system that he would have been, in-charge of. For the said job, personal **integrity** *was of paramount importance.*

What could have been done to avoid such a situation?

1. *In this case where the panel is interested to know the details of his childhood, upbringing etc. Nitin should have mentioned very transparently that he had been a happy-go-merry person till he made*

a blunder of his lifetime in 1986 and paid a heavy price for it. That thereafter he fastened his seat belts, took charge of his life, and promised never to commit such a blunder again. Nitin's frankness would have been appreciated and his strength of character would have been admired.

2. *Nitin does not need to tell about the crime he had committed and the subsequent rustication as part of his familiarization, everywhere. But all his efforts to project himself as being very popular among friends, escaping ragging by using his special skills etc. are also strictly not required.*

3. *Organizations need to do the antecedents check very thoroughly, through reliable and professional agencies, before issuing the final offer to the candidate.*

4. *In most cases, due to paucity of time, the antecedent check is done post joining of the candidate. In such cases, a self declaration, hand written by the candidate, needs to be taken before issuing the offer letter, clearly stating that the candidate understands that all information provided by her/him towards her/his candidature are true and correct in every respect. If any information is found false, s/he accepts that s/he will resign from the job immediately.*

My experience is that a few skeletons do fall out of the cupboard, while signing this declaration.

Hiring a Successor – is no big deal – until it all starts sinking,
Oh boy have I really grown old, am I becoming a past tense thing?
S/he'll be taking my chair, the morning wishes and all the salutes too,
While I'll be given a farewell and told "you have no work to do?"

Chapter Nine

Hiring a Successor

Vacancy 9	:	Regional Head-Security
Designation	:	AGM/DGM
Panel	:	Region Head, National Head Security (NHS), Head HR

STU & Co. is a very large infrastructure and service provider organization which had proclaimed its' penchant for quality, very early, by getting an appropriate ISO certification. By the nature of its' business STU & Co. has a very large asset base that is scattered across each of its' functional cells through the length and breadth of the country. These assets need to be guarded against theft and pilferage. The position isfor the Head of Security for a Region and will need to operate from the regional Headquarters–which is a State capital (in this case). The position reports into the Region Head, administratively and functionally to the National Head of Security at the Corporate Office. Retired defence personnel and ex-police officials are suited for the position. Those carrying similar experience and have maintained their physical fitness appropriately, would be preferred. Valid licence for carrying arms is necessary. Age less than 50 yrs. The grass root security is outsourced to an established agency for providing guards round-the-clock at each of the cells. Supervising their operations and ensuring their effectiveness on ground is the responsibility of the RHS. He has to also maintain healthy liaison and relationship with the local administrative authorities, so as to garner force and protection required once in a while, due to attacks from local miscreants.

Excerpts from the Interview

Candidate, Col. Jung Bahadur Singh, appears to be absolutely fit at 5 feet 11 inches height, straight taut torso with not a gram of extra flesh, chiselled tough face with small pox marks adding to his extremely masculine looks. Well dressed and polite demeanour, checked-in 15 minutes before the scheduled time and has just completed the Application Form at the reception. Col. JBS is going through the anniversary issue of the Company's house journal when he is called in to the discussion room where the panel is ready.

The National Head of Security (NHS), on the panel, Mr. Ashok Narula, has not had a defence or police background but has risen to this position over the last 25 years with the group. He joined as an Administrative Officer way back, stayed loyal to the company and is due to retire in a year. All members on the panel are aware, including Mr. Narula, that the selected candidate would also be the succeeding NHS, if he shapes-up well in the next one year.

Candidate : May I come in?

Head HR : Come in come in, you are Col.Jung Bahadur Singh?

Candidate : Yes. I am Jung Bahadur Singh. Good morning gentlemen.

NHS : Sit down Jung Bahadur. Have you brought all your documents?

Col. JBS : Well yes sir, here is my entire folio. I can provide copies of whatever is required.

(He hands over a neat plastic hard cover foolscap folder to the NHS)

NHS : What is your current CTC Jung Bahadur?

Col. JBS : (A little taken aback by the abruptness of the question)

Well, I have provided all such information in my CV.

But may I please get an introduction of all of you Gentlemen first?

Head HR : Certainly Col. He is Mr. Ashok Narula, our National Head of Security, and that is Mr. Imtiaaz Ali the Region Head for West and I am Diptamoy Goswami from HR. I have been interacting with you over phone and mails.

NHS : But what etiquettes do they teach you in the Indian Army uh! You are here for an interview and you are asking for the introduction from the panel members?

Col. JBS : (Even before I could intervene…) But what's wrong with that sir, don't we need to know each other, at least by names so that we can have a better discussion?

Reg. Head : Certainly, I agree. In fact it was our mistake we did not introduce ourselves as you came in. Shall we proceed…

NHS : Yeah, so I can see you are getting Rs.8.5 lacs in your current company. But let me be very clear to you Jung Bahadur, we will not be able to pay you as much. Our budget for the Regional Head is only 7 lacs. So are you OK with that?

Head HR : Mr. Narula, can we cut this discussion on salary and leave it to the HR to talk about, when the time comes?

First we need to know how Col. Jung Bahadur Singh can add value to our organization, please.

NHS : Your HR team does not do the screening properly DG. We will only be wasting our time with such candidates.

Col. JBS : Well even I do not like circumventing. So since this point has been brought up let me be very clear, I am looking out for a change of job only to get a more challenging role and compensation. If I do not fit into your budget let me call this off and not waste each other's precious time out here.

The candidate picks up his folio file and stands up, ready to leave.

After the candidate left the room the RH and I confronted Mr. Narula on his absolutely unprofessional behaviour. All that he had to defend himself was that after putting 25 years in this organization he has been able to reach to a salary of 8.5 lacs himself as a National Head, how can he have a Regional Head reporting into him and drawing equal if not more salary than him?

Diagnosis

The choice of members on the panel is very important not just for the interview at hand but also for the general goodwill and reputation of the company. All such public facing activities need to be very carefully handled.

Apart from that let us just have a peep into the psychology of the setting sun. It takes a lot of maturity and strength of character to look for one's own successor. Often the proposed successor would be radically different and in many ways superior and a person who has achieved more than what you have, in a shorter period of time. In case of an internal candidate (as part of succession planning) s/he would be enjoying peer level and superior level acceptance, much more than what you have been able to, in years. Unless the retiring employee has begun to switch -off, s/he would be suffering from the "halo" syndrome, that is wanting to see an equal projection one's own self in the new incumbent. While in the above case the rejection happened rather bluntly, if one would study several other similar succession hiring cases, it would be evident that getting the whole-hearted consent from the outgoing employee about her/his reliever would be very difficult. Quite obviously, why would any living being give the approval for nailing one's own coffin?

What could have been done to avoid such a situation?

Succession planning from within or bringing someone from outside does need the involvement of the current incumbent but must be done collectively by other superiors and stake-holders as well. If possible the final selection of the proposed successor must be done by significant others. The handing over of baton during the overlap period should be carefully supervised to ensure that no damage is caused during the transfer of hands, to the organizational setup.

Having said all of the above, I have myself witnessed seamless transitions (HOTO–handing over and taking over) taking place in real organizations. But the level of maturity in both, the person taking over and the one handing over, has been of par excellence levels.

Respect Them All, they are all creations of the sole Universal Creator,

Just because they have come to you for a job, they are no lesser.

The sum total of traits and skills is equal for each one of us

If only we focus on what one knows, not what one doesn't, when we assess.

Chapter Ten

Respect Them All

Vacancy10	:	Personal Assistant to Chairman
Designation	:	DM/Manager (Internal hiring–existing employees only)
Panel	:	Chairman, HR-Head

VWX & Co. had been a very traditional proprietor driven company, engaged in the conversion of chemical raw materials into intermediaries for further processing by their customers into products of mass usage. The crux of the business model was in sourcing the raw materials from the cheapest and most reliable sources and also in the management of logistics w.r.t. the finished goods. The Chairman, as an entrepreneur during the licence raj in India, had battled through the corridors of bureaucracy. He now found it very difficult to let go the reigns of his 25 years old empire to his son the designated MD–an Engineer and MBA from the US. The PA to the Chairman was a delicate position, a person with immense patience and tact was required. The PA was required to be dedicated to the Chairman, heart and soul, but could dare not ignore the rising sun, the MD. It was decided to close the position through the internal job postings, by an internal hire. Any graduate, who had spent at least 5 years in the company, could efficiently operate the computerized mailing system, take dictations over the phone, even in Hindi, but type it out in error-free English, and could manage the erratic travel schedule of the

Chairman and his family members by air, rail and/or his fleet of Mercedes,' could apply. Male candidates above 45 years were preferred as the Chairman's Office needed to be manned from 9:00 am to 11:00 pm–Monday to Friday. On Saturdays the PA would be required to travel with the Chairman up or down a few stations until he would finish signings all his papers in his special 1st AC coupe. Thereafter, the PA would have to detrain and return to base by the next return train. A rent-free house in the factory colony was part of the perks. This was also the USP for the position as a colony accommodation was considered as VIP status, with a company paid STD landline connection that came with it.

Excerpts from the Interview

This position was getting into a jinx, for me, as this was the third time that the shortlisted candidate was scheduled for the final round with the Chairman himself. In all the earlier instances the Chairman had to leave in a hurry for some unscheduled activity or the other, which had taken priority over this. The Chairman had already rejected two candidates that he had met earlier and on each instance he had added a few more parameters to his requirement for a PA. Within the limits permissible, I had requested the Chairman if I could just sit down with him once and detail out all the specific needs that he is looking for in his PA. He would very modestly decline saying "I've already told you Mr. Goswami, I am a very simple man and believe in keeping everything simple. I just need a sincere guy who has an eye for details, can check and put-up my mails and posts to me, schedule a few meetings here and there and keep track of them, take care of my travel logistics and be with me like a shadow carrying all relevant files and documents when I am visiting the various Ministries and

Govt. Offices. That's about it, Mr. Goswami. Since he may have to travel with me to Delhi sometimes and stay there in our guest house, we will provide him an accommodation here in our colony, so his family can be safe and secure and he does not have to worry about them. Is that in order Mr. Goswami and have I said anything that I did not mention to you in the earlier occasions?"

And I'd have no choice but to say, "Yes of-course Sir, I understand your requirement completely now. May I have a date and time slot that I can align some candidates for you, next week Sir?"

It was 10 o'clock at his residence in the colony that the time was scheduled for Giriraj Sharma to meet the Chairman. Third candidate and the third instance of the scheduled interview for this position, at his residence this time on a Sunday morning. If this round does not go well and as per his wish and desire, probably my understanding of the role would be questioned by none other than the Chairman and Owner of the company that I work for. Hence I was as nervous as the candidate, Giriraj, maybe more.

It was 1 o'clock now and we were still waiting. The Chairman had asked us to wait, although he was running fever and we were simply being obedient. I had a chance to talk to his wife and she only added, "No no Mr. Goswami, you are having lunch here, today. He has told me to make arrangements. He is constantly on the phone with some Ministries and Secretaries in Delhi for some licences that are getting cleared, I guess. Meanwhile I'll send another round of tea for you gentlemen."

Lunch was good, pure vegetarian, without onions and garlic too, everything made in pure deshi ghee. The aroma of the basmati rice just filled the little 40 feet by 30 feet outhouse office room that we had been sitting in. I had known Giriraj better than my wife by now, every micro details of his family, native place, his ancestors and even some details of his in-laws. Both of us had informed our families over the landline phones in the room (mobile phones had yet not come into India, then). It was time for us to inform our families once again now, not to worry about our lunch. We would probably meet them at dinner.

At about 6:30 pm our Chairman walked into the room in his satin electric blue overcoat with shining black collar and white pyjamas. With folded hands he apologised to both of us for the inordinate waiting that he had put us to, while we did feel embarrassed.

After the pleasantries, by when, he had almost completely made up for the unwarranted delay, I introduced Giriraj to our Chairman, with a few words of appreciation and the interview began.

Chairman : (In Hindi to Giriraj) Ok Sharmaji so you are a Brahmin?

Giriraj : Yes sir. Bharadwaj gotra.

Chairman : So do you follow the sanskaars, like, suryanamaskaar, sandhyaa, aachman, the navaraatras, some puja paath etc.?

Giriraj : Yes sir, within the limitations of work life balance, a little bit.

Chairman : Do you remember the Gayatri mantra? Can you narrate it for me?

Giriraj : Spells out the Gayatri mantra a little hesitantly, though.

Chairman : Your pronunciation is not quite up to the mark Giriraj, but can you now tell me the meaning of this mantra?

Giriraj : I'm sorry sir, but have forgotten the meaning–my father did teach me when I was a kid, but…

Chairman : Well that would be enough, gentlemen.

Once again I apologise for keeping you waiting for the whole day. (Stands up, and we get up from our chairs too)

You must go home now, I will discuss with you

Mr. Goswami, tomorrow morning at my office. Take care, shall I have you gentlemen dropped home?

DG : No no Sir, we have our conveyance. Take care of your health Sir, hope you recover quickly, you must take rest too.

Next Day at the Chaiman's Office:

Chairman : Well you know Mr. Goswami, I did not want to disappoint you nor the candidate. I knew after the last two instances/candidates, you would be putting up only the very best option this time. One who would be fitting my requirements 100%, if not more .

DG : Yes sir, Giriraj is actually good on all the parameters that I could evaluate him .

Chairman : I am sure he would be. But while I was talking to these Ministers and Secretaries yesterday, and my son was there in Delhi with them, all across, one of the Ministers wanted his nephew to be employed by us. He arranged for a meeting of his nephew with my son, in the afternoon. My son found him to be surprisingly very good and fitting into this role of PA for me.

DG : Well that's excellent Sir. You could have just told me that you've found somebody and that would have been enough Sir.

Chairman : No no Mr. Goswami, I could have taken Giriraj for my PA and hired the other guy in any other role. But since my son had approved and assigned him for the PA role, I did not want to deny him. I may be handing over the reigns to my son anytime now, and then Giriraj would have been in trouble, if you know what I mean…

DG : I get your point sir, I really admire your thoughtfulness. But does this new guy understand the Gayatri Mantra Sir?

Chairman : I don't know, I don't even know his name. And it really does not matter, you know that, Mr. Goswami. The reason I asked Giriraj that question is because I knew he would not know that. You must also tell him that as a young man he should learn to do things that he knows the relevance and consequence of, not just because it is customary or he has been directed to do it.

If he is reciting the mantra on a daily basis without understanding what he is doing, he may also be doing a lot of similar things in his professional life, without knowing their relevance or necessity. We need to question everything that we do and be satisfied about it. Even a child does not accept that fire is hot and can burn her/his flesh. S/he continues to explore the fire and learns to keep away from it only when s/he experiences the heat, at least once in her/his lifetime.

So tell him that he needs to focus on details and question everything that he is doing. Check out a suitable elevated role for him and take care of him after the annual appraisals this year.

DG : Amazing, I really can't believe this, Sir.

Chairman : And yes, Mr. Goswami, please take care that neither Giriraj nor anybody else talks about the selection of reference candidates, dislodging our established practice of IJPs and the fairness of our Recruitment Policy. We have not taken him just like that, you know now. My son interviewed him thoroughly and when he finally declared to me that he is good, I came out and met you people yesterday evening.

DG : Yes Sir. Thank you Sir, for so much of your valuable time and all the insights that I got from you.

Chairman : Remember Mr. Goswami, every individual is God's unique creation and needs to be respected and loved equally.

Diagnosis

Does this need any further diagnosis?

I learnt the most important lesson of HR, for my lifetime, that day:

EVERY INDIVIDUAL IS GOD'S UNIQUE CREATION AND NEEDS TO BE RESPECTED AND LOVED EQUALLY…

Epilogue

Sitting on an interview panel is a matter of great responsibility. It is invariably accompanied by the delegated authority, that of making a choice, in the best interest of the organization.

Unfortunately, it is the authority that most of us seem to get attracted to. It is that sense of being empowered to select or reject the candidates that makes the adrenaline rush for many of us. That is when we suddenly change. It is like our step-self taking over. Our dialogues with the candidates turn to first person. "I am looking for a guy who can do this that and the other…"or "I don't care whether I've to get him flown in from LA…" or "I can pay you only this much…" The moment "we" is replaced by "I," the person becomes misfit for any sensitive HR process.

I still recall the multi-billionaire Owner of a very large conglomerate and the CHRO of the same group, personally walking up twice into the guest room in their office, to apologise to me for the delay, where I was waiting for my final round of interview with them. They were getting held-up for unforeseen reasons. On the third instance, about 30 minutes swayed from the scheduled time, the CHRO again came himself to escort me in to the adjoining room and the extremely graceful Owner had stood up to receive me, while still apologizing for the delay. I was just a candidate for a State HR Head position. It did not matter to me at all, that I did not get selected, but I still recall and cherish the exemplary courteousness that was meted out and remain a strong ambassador for the organization I did not serve for even a day.

Respecting every individual for her/his accomplishments rather than evaluating what s/he lacks in, is a paradigm shift that we in India will have to undergo. And the day that happens Inshallah, interpersonal interfaces will become such an enjoyable part of our lives.

Not to say that candidates will not be rejected nor the competition will get diluted. Neither will shortcomings be brushed under the carpet. It is just the equation between a candidate and the interviewers that I am propounding to be on equal footing. It is just that the interviewer will not behave as a superior and make the candidate feel inferior. It is not a pseudo, artificial or utopian situation that I am talking about. It is simply about the fact that:

EVERY INDIVIDUAL IS GOD'S UNIQUE CREATION AND NEEDS TO BE RESPECTED AND LOVED EQUALLY…